MOTOWN
ARTIST BY ARTIST

MOTOWN
ARTIST BY ARTIST

First published in the UK in 2013

© G2 Entertainment Ltd 2014

www.G2ent.co.uk

Printed and bound in Europe

ISBN 978-1-782812-35-7

CONTENTS

Introduction

In his last professional boxing bout in Detroit's Olympia Stadium on 11 January 1950, 20-year-old featherweight Berry Gordy Jr outpointed another local fighter, Joe Nelson. Gordy, who was about to serve his country in the Korean War, had established a reputation during his 17-match career as a determined boxer who was willing to take risks to get a result. He had lost three of those 17 bouts but had won 12. It was a record that closely matched his later career in the music industry – a career that changed America.

Gordy is a winner, and in the 1960s he showed it by achieving something no one else in American history had managed: he made music that was able consistently to cross the great divide between its African-American birthplace and the mainstream of society. First the USA, then the world clicked fingers, sang along, grooved and danced to the Sound of Young America, as Gordy dubbed his wares. How could they fail to? Motown music's contagious rhythms and irresistible vocal urgings struck a universal chord and, as the US faced up to its Civil Rights responsibilities, made a nonsense of the country's history of segregation in the popular music charts and society at large.

Not that Gordy had any idea of the enormous changes America was about to go through when he borrowed $800 from his family and embarked on his Motown adventure on 12 January 1959. Aside from his boxing career he had worked in the auto industry for which his home town was famous, run a record store and written songs. He'd gained the approval of singer Jackie Wilson and recorded some of his compositions, including the renowned *Reet Petite* in 1957. Then he'd discovered a local group with grand aspirations, the Matadors, and formed a friendship with their leader, William 'Smokey' Robinson.

The Matadors became the Miracles; Robinson listened to Gordy's songwriting tips; the latter built a

portfolio of R&B artists with whom he wrote and produced. Then Robinson urged Gordy to scratch an itch that had been bothering him for some time and launch a record label: Motown Records. It took a mere nine days for Marv Johnson's *Come To Me* to be issued on the Tamla label, on 21 January 1959. The next release, featuring Wade Jones, was on the Rayber label, and then the Miracles made their Motown label debut with *Bad Girl*.

Above: *2648 West Grand Boulevard, Detroit, Michigan – the base from which Motown disseminated the Sound of Young America until 1972*

Right: Berry Gordy – invested $800 borrowed from his family to bring about a musical revolution

Motown's first taste of national success came when a song Gordy had co-written, *Money (That's What I Want)*, was recorded by Barrett Strong and released in August 1959. Initially issued on the Tamla label, it was picked up by Anna Records (started by Gordy's sisters Anna and Gwen) and hit number two on the R&B chart and 23 on the Billboard Hot 100. Motown was getting up a head of steam, but Gordy had to wait until September 1960 for the Miracles' *Shop Around* (Tamla) to go all the way to the top of the R&B chart and tantalisingly close to the peak of the pop listings.

By that time Gordy had bought the white-framed house at 2648 West Grand Boulevard that was to be the home of his Motown operation until 1972. Showing typical audacity, he had a sign proclaiming the building as 'Hitsville USA' affixed over the front door – a claim whose accuracy was to be proved many times over. The garage was converted into a studio, and it was there that *Shop Around* and countless other hits were recorded.

The Motown stable was growing as talented young artists from Detroit's working class joined in the race to be the first to reach number one on the pop chart. That honour went to the Marvelettes, whose 1961 song *Please Mr Postman* had been co-written by a young Brian Holland. Meanwhile, Gordy was busy building Motown into an independent hit factory that would rival and even exceed the output of the huge corporations.

There were whispers in the 60s that he had modelled Motown's slick processes on the assembly lines of Detroit's car manufacturers: having found a good product he turned out similar ones, and did it quickly. All the elements of music factory production were there: the in-house songwriting and production units like Robinson and Holland-Dozier-Holland; the house musicians and support singers; the performing geniuses – Marvin Gaye, 'Little' Stevie Wonder, Mary Wells, the male and female vocal groups like the Temptations and the Supremes; the weekly 'quality control' meetings.

But however the music was produced, it was fresh and glorious and it was played on millions of transistor radios, making Motown into a phenomenon the like of which the world had never seen and has not seen since. Motown took the rhythms and the call-and-

Above: *Berry Gordy Jr Boulevard – Detroit thoroughfare named after Motown's founding father*

response formats of African-American music forms and transformed them with superb melodies, memorable lyrics, brilliant musicianship, handclaps, wailing singers, blasting horns and driving bass and drums. *Where Did Our Love Go, Dancing In The Street, Get Ready, Reach Out …* hit succeeded hit as the stars illuminated the 60s.

Britons took to the Motown sound like ducks to water, getting their fixes on the Tamla-Motown label from 1965 and sometimes making stars of artists who struggled in the States. That label was just one of many that Gordy introduced over the years to spread and diversify his message: Gordy, Miracle, Soul, VIP, Mel-o-dy and Rare Earth were just a few.

Motown changed; of course it did. Artists and backroom teams came and went, and in 1972 the company aided its expansion into the wider entertainment industry by moving to Los Angeles. The company evolved with the changing times in the 70s and 80s and then, in 1988, Gordy sold his holding in Motown to MCA Records. The label kept producing world-class music, though, even when ownership passed to Polydor in 1994. Nowadays the light is kept burning under the Universal Motown banner.

Motown celebrated its 50th anniversary in 2009, marking the occasion with a huge reissue exercise that saw much of its stupendous back catalogue introduced to new generations. So the records that got feet moving in the 60s continue to do so.

7o2

Right: *702 – Las Vegas sisters with the platinum touch*

Stand-up comedian Sinbad discovered sisters LeMisha, Orish and Irish Grinstead singing in the lobby of the Caesars Palace casino in Las Vegas. He sent them to a talent show in Atlanta, Georgia, where Michael Bivins of R&B group New Edition liked what he saw. After their recorded debut, with cousin Amelia Childs, on Subway's hit single *This Lil' Game We Play*, Kameelah Williams replaced Amelia. Orish came and went from the group – she was to die aged 27 in 2008 – but, with the help of Missy 'Misdemeanour' Elliott, work started on the group's first album, *No Doubt* (1996). The album yielded three hit singles, earned the group a *Soul Train* Lady of Soul Award and sold more than half a million copies worldwide. Missy Elliott produced 702's biggest hit, *Where My Girls At?*, which stayed on the Billboard Hot 100 chart for more than 30 weeks. The album from which it came, *702*, has been certified platinum and the group's third, *Star* (2003), also earned heavy sales. Further exposure came when they recorded the lead single, *Pootie Tangin'*, for the Chris Rock film *Pootie Tang*. The group's biggest UK hit came from their performance on *Beep Me 911*, taken from Missy Elliott's 1997 album *Supa Dupa Fly*. In 2010, Kameelah confirmed that she would continue her solo career.

Founded: 1994
Origin: Las Vegas, Nevada
Type: R&B, soul, hip hop
Members: Amelia Childs, Irish Grinstead, LeMisha Grinstead, Orish Grinstead, Cree Lamore, Kameelah Williams
Highest chart positions: 4 US (*Where My Girls At*, 1999); 14 UK (*Beep Me 911,* 1998)

98 Degrees

Four Ohio boys got together on the West Coast to form the sweet soul quartet 98 Degrees (stylised as 98°), and were given the chance to sing on a local radio station after trying to crash the backstage area of a Boyz II Men show. Before long the group had signed to Motown and hit the charts with their debut single, *Invisible Man* (1997). The first, self-titled album was followed by three others, with the singles *Because of You* and *The Hardest Thing* surging higher up the charts. But they were surpassed by *Thank God I Found You*, the Mariah Carey song on which the group guested with singer Joe, and *Give Me Just One Night (Una Noche)*, which hit the number two spot on the Hot 100. In 2002 the band announced that they were in hiatus – they were still a band but would work on solo projects. Nick Lachey was married, briefly, to fellow pop star Jessica Simpson and became a TV star; others also wound up in television work. It was a long break, but the band eventually got together again

in 2012 and released an album, *98° 2.0*, in May 2013. It was their first album since *Revelation*, which reached number two in the US chart in 2000.

Above: *98 Degrees – made the most of a chance to sing on local radio*

Founded: 1996

Origin: Los Angeles, California

Type: R&B, soul, pop

Members: Drew Lachey, Nick Lachey, Justin Jeffre, Jeff Timmons

Highest chart positions: 1 US (*Thank God I Found You*, 2000); 10 UK (*Thank God I Found You*)

Luther Allison

LUTHER ALLISON

Below:
*Luther Allison
– transformed
Chicago blues*

Luther Allison was the first blues musician to sign to Motown, and he remains one of very few. The 14th of 15 children born to Arkansas cotton farmers, he developed his skills after the family moved to Chicago, playing bass in guitarist Jimmy Dawkins' band and listening to blues greats like Freddie King, Otis Rush and Buddy Guy. Soon he was sitting in with the likes of the legendary Muddy Waters, Howlin' Wolf and Elmore James. Allison's first album, *Love Me Mama*, was released in 1969 and his live shows to promote the record, showcasing the soul-filled vocals and lengthy guitar solos that were likened in some quarters to those of Jimi Hendrix, became legendary. He managed to take Chicago blues and transform them with inventive touches of jazz, rock, funk, soul, even reggae, into something original. He signed to Motown in 1972 and released two albums – *Bad News Is Coming* (1972) and *Luther's Blues* (1974) – that have been hailed as masterpieces and another, *Night Life* (1976), that was not so well received. Allison was never going to trouble the record charts, but by the end of his stint with Motown he was touring worldwide and had become a great favourite of festival-goers, especially in Europe. In 1992 he even played 18 dates with French legend Johnny Hallyday, having lived in France since the 70s. In 1996 Motown reissued the material Allison had recorded for the label, but the following year he succumbed to lung cancer at the age of 57.

Born: 17 August 1939, Widener, Arkansas
Died: 12 August 1997, Madison, Wisconsin
Type: Blues

Gerald Alston

As did so many Motown artists, Gerald Alston learned his trade in church, and he has an impeccable pedigree: he is a nephew of Johnny Fields (founding member of the Five Blind Boys of Alabama) and of Shirley Alston Reeves, lead singer of the Shirelles. He formed the New Imperials, performing both religious and secular music, while in his teens and at one show the Manhattans arranged to borrow some equipment from the band. They heard the 17-year-old Alston singing when they arrived to pick it up and asked him to join. Before he took over the lead vocal role in 1971, the Manhattans had had several minor hits; with Alston up front they were transformed into bigger stars, marking up regular top 50 appearances, hitting new highs with *Kiss And Say Goodbye* and earning a Grammy in 1980 for *Shining Star*. Alston signed for Motown and went solo in 1988, and continued to make a mark. His self-titled debut album (1988) and *Always In The Mood* (1992) earned praise and *Take Me Where You* *Want To* (1988) and *Slow Motion* (1990) took him to number three in the R&B charts. By 1995 he was back in familiar territory with the Manhattans, and the band continues to tour and record.

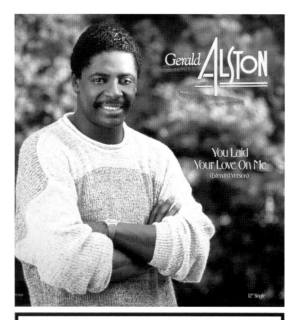

Gerald ALSTON
You Laid
Your Love On Me
(Extended Version)

12" Single

Left: *Gerald Alston – rejoined the Manhattans after a solo career*

Born: 8 November 1951, North Carolina
Type: R&B, soul
Highest chart positions: 1 US with the Manhattans (*Kiss And Say Goodbye*, 1976); 4 UK with the Manhattans (*Hurt*, 1975 and *Kiss And Say Goodbye*)

The Andantes

Think of a Motown hit in the 1960s; there's a pretty good chance the Andantes sang on it. Marlene Barrow, Louvain Demps and Jackie Hicks were the background vocals trio that the producers went to when they were planning their sessions and wanted top quality. They say they appeared on more than 20,000 sessions; it's just a tragedy that Motown saw fit to release just one of their own records, 1964's *(Like A) Nightmare*. Otherwise, from 1962 onwards they graced classics by the likes of the Temptations, Martha Reeves & the Vandellas, the Supremes, the Four Tops, Marvin Gaye, Stevie Wonder, Jimmy Ruffin, Edwin Starr and the Marvelettes. When the Motown A-team of Holland-Dozier-Holland was in charge of a session, especially for the Four Tops, the Andantes wouldn't be far away. And the bosses weren't averse to using the group as studio substitutes for stars like Mary Wilson and Cindy Birdsong of the Supremes, the whole of the Vandellas and most of the Marvelettes. Fame in the shape of Motown's biggest performers was never far away, but it wasn't to touch the Andantes directly.

Founded: 1960
Origin: Detroit, Michigan
Type: R&B, soul, pop, disco
Members: Marlene Barrow, Louvain Demps, Jackie Hicks, Pat Lewis
Highest chart positions: 1 US with Mary Wells (*My Guy*, 1964), with the Four Tops (*I Can't Help Myself (Sugar Pie, Honey Bunch)*, 1965, *Reach Out I'll Be There*, 1966), with Diana Ross & the Supremes (*Love Child*, 1968), with Marvin Gaye (*I Heard It Through The Grapevine*, 1968); 1 UK with the Supremes (*Baby Love*, 1964), *Reach Out I'll Be There, I Heard It Through The Grapevine*

Another Bad Creation

Sometimes abbreviated to ABC, the preteen quintet Another Bad Creation were discovered by Michael Bivins, founder of the Boston R&B group New Edition and hip hop outfit Bell Biv Devoe. The young group struck platinum with their first album release on Motown, 1991's *Coolin' at the Playground Ya' Know*, which peaked at number seven on the Billboard 200 and, according to at least one observer, helped to reaffirm Motown's status as the dominant force in R&B. The album yielded no fewer than five singles, and two of them, *Iesha* and *Playground*, broke into the top 10. It was no surprise that Bivins had a hand in the writing of both of the hits, or that Another Bad Creation should cover the New Edition song *Jealous Girl*, which reached 25 on the R&B chart. The group's Mark and Dave capitalised on their celebrity by appearing in Michael Jackson's *Black Or White* video and all five of them featured in the movie *The Meteor Man*, dyeing their hair blonde for the occasion. The second album, *It Ain't What U Wear, It's How U Play It*, followed in 1993 but failed to follow up on the million-selling success of the first, and the group broke up soon afterwards. Despite the hype, they had not become the next Jackson 5.

Left: *Another Bad Creation – it wasn't what they wore, it was how they played it*

Founded: 1988
Origin: Atlanta, Georgia
Type: R&B, rap, hip hop, new jack swing
Members: Romell 'RoRo' Chapman, Demetrius 'Red' Pugh, Marliss 'Mark' Pugh, Chris Sellers, David Shelton, Adrian 'GA' Witcher
Highest chart positions: 9 US (*Iesha*, 1990); 4 US R&B (*Playground*, 1991)

Ashford & Simpson

Below: *Ashford & Simpson – as songwriters and performers, they were as solid as a rock*

Whether as songwriters and producers or as performers, the husband–and–wife team of Ashford & Simpson served Motown royally from the 1960s onwards, serving up hit after hit and being rewarded by their induction into the Songwriters Hall of Fame in 2002. After writing for artists like Ray Charles, Aretha Franklin and the 5th Dimension, the couple were lured on to the Motown staff by Berry Gordy and were paired with Marvin Gaye and Tammi Terrell. The hits that followed included *Ain't No Mountain High Enough* and *You're All I Need To Get By*. Work with Diana Ross, Gladys Knight & the Pips, Smokey Robinson & the Miracles, the Marvelettes and the Dynamic Superiors yielded many another hit, including Ross's *Reach Out And Touch (Somebody's Hand)*. Ashford, working with Frank Wilson

this time, produced the 1968 smash *I'm Going To Make You Love Me* for Diana Ross & the Supremes and the Temptations. As performers, Ashford & Simpson's career had begun in the early 1960s in the gospel group the Followers and developed with work with Quincy Jones and others. Simpson recorded two albums for Motown in 1971 and 1972 – *Exposed* and *Valerie Simpson* – but it wasn't until the couple had left Motown for Warner Bros and then Capitol that they found the recording success as a duo that they deserved. Their marriage, celebrated in 1974, was cut short by Ashford's death from throat cancer complications in 2011.

Founded: 1964
Origin: New York City
Type: R&B, soul, disco, gospel
Members: Nickolas Ashford, Valerie Simpson
Highest chart positions: 12 US, 1 US R&B (*Solid (As A Rock), 1984*); 3 UK (*Solid (As A Rock)*)

Erykah Badu

Erica Wright, better known as Erykah Badu or the Queen of Neo-Soul, has done it all, pretty much. She's a singer-songwriter, an actress, a community activist, a teacher, a record producer, an innovator and, among all that, the mother of three children. She's known for the video of *Window Seat*, shot in Dealey Plaza in Dallas, the site of John F Kennedy's assassination, in which she shed clothes as she walked until she was naked. But she's famed primarily for her distinctive singing, which has drawn comparisons with jazz legend Billie Holiday but is decidedly of today. Her first album for Motown, *Mama's Gun* (2000) followed initial success on the R&B and album charts, especially with the ground-breaking *Baduizm* (1997), for which she wrote all but one of the songs. *Mama's Gun* contained the big hit *Bag Lady*. Three further albums have followed, all of them critically acclaimed: *Worldwide Underground* (2003), *New Amerykah Part One (4th World War)* (2008) and, in 2010, *New Amerykah*

Part Two (Return Of The Ankh). The first of the 'New Amerykah' releases was a concept album that covered the themes of poverty, urban violence, cultural identity and complacency, while the second focused on the more usual subjects of romance and relationships and provided the controversial *Window Seat*. The next offering is eagerly awaited.

Born: 26 February 1971, Dallas, Texas
Type: R&B, soul, funk, jazz, hip hop
Highest chart positions: 6 US, 1 US R&B (*Bag Lady*, 2000); 1 US R&B (*On & On*, 1996, *Tyrone*, 1997, *Love Of My Life (An Ode To Hip-Hop)*, 2002); 12 UK (*On & On*)

JJ Barnes

Right: *JJ Barnes – big name on the Northern Soul circuit*

James Jay Barnes never threatened the mainstream charts much on either side of the Atlantic. But he was (and his records remain) a major feature of the UK's Northern Soul scene, where several of his songs have long been established floor-fillers. It was thanks to the Tamla-Motown label, which brought Motown music to the British masses through its distribution deal with EMI, that Barnes found the success he missed out on in the States. He cut his first record, *My Love Came Tumbling Down*, when he was 17 in 1960 but, like his other early releases, they found no great favour – except later, with the Northern Soul crowd. His biggest hit came in 1967, when *Baby Please Come Back Home*, co-written by Barnes with Detroit writer-producer Don Davis, delighted young America and became a huge favourite in the country's skating rinks, but he failed to find a follow-up. Treading in his friend Edwin Starr's footsteps towards England in the 1970s, he became a star. Tamla-Motown re-released early recordings like *Please Let Me In* and *Real Humdinger* to please the denizens of the dance clubs in northern England, like Manchester's the Twisted Wheel, who craved sounds from Motown and rarer US labels. The 1980s saw Barnes releasing records including a version of *Do I Love You (Indeed I Do)*, a Northern soul favourite originally recorded by Motown songwriter and producer Frank Wilson.

Born: 30 November 1943, Detroit, Michigan
Type: R&B, soul, pop
Highest chart positions: 61 US, 9 US R&B (*Baby Please Come Back Home*, 1967)

The Boys

The oldest of the Abdulsamad brothers, Khiry, was only 15 when *Dial My Heart* hit the top of the US R&B charts in the winter of 1988. The youngest, Bilal, was still only 15 when the group's career ground to a halt in 1993. In between, the Boys released three albums and 10 singles on Motown, toured widely, appeared on Michael Jackson's *Moonwalk* video, recorded with Earth, Wind & Fire and had their own TV show. The act, which started with the brothers trying to earn some cash for a Father's Day present on the beach at Venice, California, drove audiences wild with snappy dance routines and stunning acrobatics combined with exhilarating vocals. The Boys, despite their youth, co-wrote and produced their own records and were astutely managed by their parents, who had studied specifically to promote their offspring. It seemed to be going well up to the point when *Crazy* topped the R&B charts and breached the top 30 on the Billboard Hot 100, but the hits started to tail off. They stopped completely when the Boys refused a new Motown contract.

Later in the 1990s, they moved to Gambia in West Africa, where they set up a studio and started to work under the name of the Suns of Light. It's a long way from those early gigs on the beach.

Left: *The Boys – snappy dance routines and stunning acrobatics*

Founded: 1984

Origin: Carson, California

Type: pop, new jack swing

Members: Bilal Abdulsamad, Hakim Abdulsamad, Khiry Abdulsamad, Tajh Abdulsamad

Highest chart positions: 13 US, 1 US R&B (*Dial My Heart*, 1988); 1 US R&B (*Lucky Charm*, 1989, *Crazy*, 1990)

Boyz II Men

BOYZ II MEN

Below: *Boyz II Men – perhaps the most commercially successful R&B group of the modern era*

They've never been quite as big in the UK as they are on the other side of the pond, but in the USA Boyz II Men's numbers are impressive: the Record Industry Association of America calculates that they're the most commercially successful R&B group in history. And the best, most hit-filled years of Boyz II Men's mega-selling career came when they were with Motown. It all started at the Philadelphia High School for Creative and Performing Arts, where the original quartet of Nate and Wanya Morris, Marc Nelson and Michael McCary practised their razor-sharp harmonies and fell in with the influential New Edition member Michael Bivins. He it was who, in 1991, produced the first Motown album, *Cooleyhighharmony*, which soared to number three in the US and

seven in the UK. The two succeeding albums, *II* and *Evolution*, went all the way to the top. On the singles front, *End Of The Road* was a worldwide chart-topper and it sparked a golden run that saw the group register numerous top 10 successes. After 1997's *A Song For Mama* and the departure from Motown, however, hits have been harder to find, *Thank You In Advance* (2000) being the only single to break into the Hot 100.

Founded: 1988
Origin: Philadelphia, Pennsylvania
Type: R&B, new jack swing, soul
Members: Michael McCary, Nathan Morris, Wanya Morris, Mark Nelson, Shawn Stockman
Highest chart positions: 1 US, 1 US R&B (*End Of The Road*, 1992, *I'll Make Love To You*, 1994); 1 US (*On Bended Knee*, 1994, *4 Seasons Of Loneliness*, 1997); 1 US R&B (*It's So Hard To Say Goodbye To Yesterday* and *Uhh Ahh*, both 1991, *A Song For Mama*, 1997); 1 UK (*End Of The Road*)

Johnny Bristol

Johnny Bristol became a real part of the Motown family when he married the label's Vice-President Iris Gordy, but it was his singing and writing for the label that made his name. He started out in 1960 as half of Johnny and Jackie, with Jackie Beavers, and the duo cut the first version of *Someday We'll Be Together* (later to become a hit for the Supremes) for Gwen Gordy and Harvey Fuqua's Tri-Phi label. Tri-Phi was absorbed by Motown and Bristol stayed at Hitsville throughout the 60s, working with Fuqua and writing and producing for artists like Diana Ross, Stevie Wonder, Marvin Gaye and Smokey Robinson. The pair's production credits included *Ain't No Mountain High Enough* and *If I Could Build My Whole World Around You* for Gaye and Tammi Terrell and *My Whole World Ended (The Moment You Left Me)* for David Ruffin. Bristol is known as the producer and co-writer of the final hit singles of both Diana Ross & the Supremes (*Someday We'll Be Together*) and Smokey Robinson & the Miracles

(*We've Come Too Far To End It Now*) before their lead singers departed. His was the male voice on that Supremes record, and he was to find a modicum of solo success when he left Motown in 1973, *Hang On In There Baby* scoring on both sides of the Atlantic.

Left: *Johnny Bristol – hung on in there to have hits on both sides of the pond*

Born: 3 February 1939, Morganton, North Carolina
Died: 21 March 2004, Brighton Township, Michigan
Type: R&B, soul
Highest chart positions: 8 US, 2 US R&B (*Hang On In There Baby*, 1974); 3 UK (*Hang On In There Baby*)

Chris Clark

Motown hasn't had too many white stars but Chris Clark's blue-eyed soul vocals made her a natural, and she has broken new ground for the label in terms of the longevity of her career. Berry Gordy is said to have hated the songs the 18-year-old singer presented to him on a demo but was drawn to her voice, which was perfect for her raunchy debut *Do Right Baby, Do Right* in 1966. The same year saw Clark break into the R&B charts with *Love's Gone Bad*, written by Holland-Dozier-Holland. It wasn't long before Clark and Gordy were working together as a creative team (as well as on a personal level), and their songwriting collaboration included *I Want To Go Back There Again*. Her interracial relationship with Gordy was sadly too often a touchy subject in the USA, but Clark was welcomed in the UK, where she released a series of singles that mysteriously never troubled the charts. The aforementioned *I Want To Go Back There Again* and *Whisper You Love Me Boy* were among them. A six-foot platinum blonde who could belt out R&B with the best of them, she presented a striking figure on stage, but it was in the background that Clark spent the last days of her Motown career, having gained an Oscar nomination for her work on the screenplay of the Diana Ross vehicle *Lady Sings The Blues*.

Born: 1 February 1946, Santa Cruz, California
Type: soul, R&B
Highest chart position: 41 US R&B (*Love's Gone Bad*, 1966)

Tom Clay

Born under the name of Clague, Tom Clay was well known on the airwaves of Detroit in the 1950s and 1960s and became as popular a personality off the radio as on it. His Jack the Bellboy character, aired on the WJBK-AM station, endeared him to the listeners of Motor City and ensured he would draw crowds to the record hops that featured artists of the day. Fired for taking money in return for playing records in a payola scandal in 1959, he re-established himself in Canada but left his station in the wake of another dubious scheme: his Beatles Booster Club offered merchandise in exchange for a dollar but seldom delivered. Clay moved back to Detroit before landing at Los Angeles station KGBS in 1971. Here he put together the record that made his name: a medley of Bacharach-David's *What The World Needs Now Is Love* and Dick Holler's *Abraham, Martin And John* interspersed with snatches of news reports on the assassinations of John and Robert Kennedy and Martin Luther King Jr. Beginning with a recording of a little girl answering questions on segregation, bigotry and hatred, the record hit a nerve and sold over a million when it was released on Motown's MoWest label. Clay tried again with *Whatever Happened To* but his recording career was over; he remains one of a select band of one-hit wonders.

Left: *Martin Luther King Jr – speech was captured on Tom Clay's only hit*

Born: 20 August 1929, New York
Died: 22 November 1995, Los Angeles, California
Type: disc jockey
Highest chart positions: 8 US, 32 US R&B (*What The World Needs Now Is Love/Abraham, Martin And John*, 1971)

The Commodores

There aren't many more celebrated Motown acts than the Commodores, who chalked up seven number one hits in the US R&B charts, entered the top 10 of the Billboard Hot 100 no fewer than 10 times and penetrated the upper reaches of the UK chart five times. They launched the phenomenon that is the career of Lionel Richie, too. The story began when two Tuskegee groups, the Mystics and the Jays, broke up and Richie got together with William King, Thomas McClary, Ronald LaPread, Walter 'Clyde' Orange and Milan Williams to form a new band. Stuck for

a name, they picked a word out of the dictionary and struck out for New York City where friends and family packed out a gig, persuading the delighted promoter to book the group for two weeks. In 1971 the Commodores auditioned in New York for a gig that promised precious exposure to a mass audience, not knowing that it entailed providing support on a Jackson 5 tour. The gig lasted for two years and led to the Commodores signing for the Jacksons' label, Motown. Keyboard player Williams' lively instrumental *Machine Gun* was the group's first release, and it surprised no one when it made the top 30. Further progress came with the release of *I Feel Sanctified* and the band's first number one record on the R&B chart, 1975's *Slippery When Wet*. America and Britain had taken to their special brand of funk and soul, with Richie and Orange delivering in style in the vocal department. The hits continued to arrive, but the sound took a different direction with the 1977 release

of *Easy*, a chart-topper with a laid-back feel that has charmed listeners ever since and, at the time, signalled to the band that the production of silky ballads might be the route to take. *Still* (1979), written by Richie, proved to be one of the band's most memorable numbers, hitting number one in the States and four in the UK, but it was also the last major hit to feature the singer. Richie cut *Endless Love* with label-mate Diana Ross in 1981, mapping out the road he was to take when he left the Commodores the following year. JD Nicholas, formerly of Heatwave, filled Richie's shoes and it was with him that the band recorded *Nightshift*, their last single to reach the top spot in the R&B charts. Written by Orange, Dennis Lambert and Franne Golde, it was a poignant tribute to fellow musicians Jackie Wilson and Marvin Gaye, and it won the band a Grammy. The Motown days came to an end in 1985 and the Commodores eventually formed their own label, but they were never again to reach the heights they had touched with the people who had picked them for that Jackson 5 tour.

Founded: 1968
Origin: Tuskegee, Alabama
Type: Funk, soul
Members: Charles Dean, William King, Ronald LaPread, Thomas McClary, JD Nicholas, Walter Orange, Sheldon Reynolds, Lionel Richie, Milan Williams
Highest chart positions: 1 US, 1 US R&B (*Three Times A Lady*, 1978, *Still*, 1979); 1 US R&B (*Slippery When Wet*, 1975, *Just To Be Close To You*, 1976, *Easy*, 1977, *Too Hot Ta Trot*, 1978, *Nightshift*, 1985); 1 UK (*Three Times A Lady*)

The Contours

Below: *The Contours – raw approach somewhat at odds with the smooth Motown sound*

Starting life as a quartet named the Blenders, the Contours recruited new members and were soon making a splash with their exuberant stage act and masterly choreography. Motown boss Berry Gordy wasn't convinced at first but the group persevered, enlisting the help of soul star Jackie Wilson, cousin of band member Hubert Johnson. Finally Gordy conceded, signing the group in 1961. For a second single release, on his subsidiary Gordy Records label, he offered them *Do You Love Me?*, a raucous number that was unsuited to most Motown acts, and it roared to the top of the R&B charts. Although the group's raw approach was somewhat out of kilter with the fast-developing, silky smooth, classic Motown sound, further hits followed in the form of *Shake*

Sherrie (1963), *Can You Jerk Like Me?* (1964), *The Day When She Needed Me* (1964), *First I Look At The Purse* (1965) and *Just A Little Misunderstanding* (1966). The last single to chart was *It's So Hard Being A Loser* (1967), by which time the group were suffering from their incompatibility with the Motown norm. In 1987 *Do You Love Me?* resurfaced on the soundtrack of the movie *Dirty Dancing*, giving the Contours a last glimpse of chart fame, although versions of the band continue to tour.

Founded: 1958

Origin: Detroit, Michigan

Type: R&B

Members: Joe Billingslea, Huey Davis, Dennis Edwards, Council Gay, Billy Gordon, Kim Green, Billy Hogg, Hubert Johnson, Sylvester Potts, Joe Stubbs, Tony Womack

Highest chart positions: 3 US, 1 US R&B (*Do You Love Me?*, 1962); 31 UK (*Just A Little Misunderstanding*, 1966)

Dazz Band

Taking their name from the mingling of the words danceable and jazz, Cleveland's Dazz Band had their origins in two funk ensembles by the names of Bell Telefunk and Mother Braintree. What emerged was an eight-piece that majored on funk and made a sizeable impression on the audiences of the early 1980s. They had already had two minor hits (under the name of Kinsman Dazz) when they signed to Motown in 1980 and released their first album, *Invitation to Love*. The following year saw them start to make inroads on the charts, but it was in 1982 that their biggest hit, *Let It Whip*, rose to number five on the Hot 100. Taken from the third album, *Keep It Live*, it also reaped the group a Grammy Award for the best performance by an R&B vocal group. While further hit singles followed – notably *Joystick* (1983), which saw the band adopting hip hop production techniques and preferring drum machines and keyboards to horns – Dazz Band's albums were what mostly kept them in the public eye while they remained at Motown. *Hot Spot* (1985) and *Wild & Free* (1986) peaked at 114 and 178 respectively in the Billboard 200, but the latter was the band's last chart placement. A change of label had done them no favours, it seemed.

Left: *Dazz Band – majored on funk and earned a Grammy Award*

Founded: 1977
Origin: Cleveland, Ohio
Type: R&B, funk
Members: Pierre DeMudd, Eric Fearman, Kevin Frederick, Bobby Harris, Keith Harrison, Skip Martin, Marlon McClain, Kenny Pettus, Isaac Wiley Jr, Michael Wiley
Highest chart positions: 5 US, 1 US R&B (*Let It Whip*, 1982)

Debbie Dean

It had to be someone, and it turned out to be Debbie Dean, otherwise known as Reba Jeanette Smith (her birth name), Penny Smith, Debra Dion and Debbie Stevens: she was the first white artist to be signed by Berry Gordy to his young label. Dean had previously recorded for ABC Paramount and Roulette Records when she moved over to Motown in 1960, kick-starting her career at Hitsville USA with the single *Itty Bitty Pity Love* in August 1961. It was not a success, and neither was the next release, conceived as an answer to the Miracles' number two hit *Shop Around*. Despite being written by the combined talents of Gordy, Smokey Robinson and Loucye Wakefield, *Don't Let Him Shop Around*, released a month after Dean's first single, bombed. She was inhibited by several disadvantages, not least of which was her age, 34 when her third Motown single, *Everybody's Talking About Me* (1962), became her third to fail. She moved to California, where she met Motown-affiliated songwriter/producer Deke Richards, and the pair hit it off as a writing partnership. Together they came up with songs such as *I'm Gonna Make It (I Will Wait For You)* and *Honey Bee (Keep On Stinging Me)* for the Supremes, *I Can't Dance To That Music You're Playing* for Martha Reeves & the Vandellas and *Sweet Joy Of Life* for Edwin Starr. Motown's first white artist had found her niche.

Born: 1 February 1928, Corbin, Kentucky
Died: 17 February 2001, Ojai, California
Type: R&B, soul, doo-wop

DeBarge

Left: *DeBarge – it was strictly a family affair*

For a while, it looked as if the DeBarge siblings might do for Motown what their counterparts in the Jackson family had already done: reap platinum success time after time. That was, it turned out, a bit too much to ask, but DeBarge did gain a place in the hearts of music lovers worldwide and give rise to a family franchise that still delights. Signing with Motown and thus following in the footsteps of older brothers Tommy and Bobby (who were in the Motown band Switch), DeBarge debuted with the album *The DeBarges* in 1981. It was the following year, however, that the follow-up *All This Love* struck gold and the hit singles started to flow. *I Like It, All This Love, Time Will Reveal* and *Love Me In A Special Way* all charted, and they were followed by a global smash, *Rhythm Of The Night*. Written by Diane Warren (whose songwriting career it kick-started), the song benefited from its inclusion in the Motown movie *The Last Dragon* and showcased El DeBarge's tenor/falsetto range. The next single,

Who's Holding Donna Now (1985), reached number six in the US, but thereafter the band's fortunes declined with the departure of El to pursue solo fame. It was the end of DeBarge, but not of the DeBarges.

Founded: 1978

Origin: Grand Rapids, Michigan

Type: R&B, soul, funk, pop, adult contemporary

Members: Bobby DeBarge, Bunny DeBarge, El DeBarge, James DeBarge, Mark DeBarge, Randy DeBarge

Highest chart positions: 3 US, 1 US R&B (*Rhythm Of The Night*, 1985); 1 US R&B (*Time Will Reveal*, 1983); 4 UK (*Rhythm Of The Night*)

Chico DeBarge

As the recording career of Bobby, Bunny, James, Mark and Randy under the band name of DeBarge was winding down, that of younger brother Chico (born Jonathan Arthur) was just beginning. Signing to Motown in the mid-80s, he released a self-titled album in 1986 that provoked interest and gave rise to his biggest single, *Talk To Me*. A further cut from the album, *The Girl Next Door*, charted, but much lower. For his next album, *Kiss Serious*, Chico enlisted the production help of Brownmark, bass player with Prince & the Revolution, and the funk influence showed. The biggest-selling single, *Rainy Nights*, hit number 18 on the R&B

charts. Not long after, Chico and brother Bobby were arrested and convicted of trafficking cocaine, and they received six-year prison sentences. From adversity came good things, however: Chico used his time inside wisely, growing as a musician and writing. On his release from jail in the mid-90s, he returned to Motown and found himself under the wing of the president of the time, Kedar Massenburg, and benefiting from his neo soul initiative Kedar Entertainment. The 1997 album *Long Time No See* spawned the singles *Virgin* and *Soopaman Lover*, and it was followed in 1999 by the autobiographical *The Game*, which told the story of an ex-con struggling to stay straight. Chico continued to work despite drug problems, with his latest album release coming in 2009.

Born: 23 June 1966, Detroit, Michigan
Type: R&B, soul, pop, hip hop
Highest chart positions: 21 US, 7 US R&B (*Talk To Me*, 1986); UK 50 (*Iggin' Me*, 1997)

El DeBarge

El DeBarge (born Eldra Patrick) is the sixth of the 10 singing DeBarges, and the best-known of them all. His was the distinctive falsetto most often heard on the group's hits like *Love Me In A Special Way* and *Rhythm Of The Night*, and he is the one who has carved out the most successful solo career. El left the band in 1986 and released his first solo album, simply called *El DeBarge*, the same year on the Gordy label. From it came his biggest hit on both sides of the Atlantic, *Who's Johnny*, which was used in the comedy science fiction film *Short Circuit* and topped the US R&B charts. The memorable video featured El singing in a courtroom in which the movie's robotic protagonist is on trial. The album also yielded the lesser-known charting singles *Love Always* and *Someone*. El fans had to wait three years for his second album, *Gemini*, released on the Motown label this time. It was a critical and commercial failure, however, and his days with Motown were numbered. His contract was terminated in 1990 and he went to

Above: *El DeBarge – courtroom video capitalised on the sci-fi film Short Circuit*

work for Warner Bros, but the days of mainstream chart success were finished. While he struggled with problems arising from drug use, El appeared sporadically in the R&B charts, but there was a 16-year gap between albums, ended by the 2010 release of *Second Chance*.

Born: 4 June 1961, Detroit, Michigan
Type: R&B, soul, dance-pop
Highest chart positions: 3 US, 1 US R&B (*Who's Johnny*, 1986); UK 60 (*Who's Johnny*)

Kiki Dee

For a long time in the 1960s and 1970s, Kiki Dee (born Pauline Matthews) was Britain's best-kept pop secret. She finally came to the prominence that her immense talent deserved with the monster 1976 hit *Don't Go Breaking My Heart*, sung as a duo with Elton John on the latter's Rocket label. But Motown bosses had recognised Dee's gifts much earlier, making her the first white Briton – indeed the first European – to sign to the label. She had paid her dues with a Bradford dance band, as a session singer and providing backing vocals for Dusty Springfield, and she achieved acclaim – but no chart status –

with singles such as 1965's *Why Don't I Run Away From You* (a favourite on pirate radio stations) and the 1968 B-side *On A Magic Carpet Ride*, which is still a staple on the Northern Soul circuit. Signing to a Tamla-Motown/EMI deal in 1970, Dee first released the single *The Day Will Come Between Sunday and Monday* and then, in 1971 on Motown's Rare Earth label, *Love Makes The World Go Round*. Sadly and unjustly, neither record found favour with the public, and neither did the album from which they came. *Great Expectations* featured favourites like *My Whole World Ended (The Moment You Left Me)* and *I Second That Emotion* but hardly registered. It took Elton John to launch Dee to fame on a Rocket.

Born: 6 March 1947, Bradford, West Yorkshire
Type: Soul, pop
Highest chart positions: 1 US (*Don't Go Breaking My Heart* with Elton John, 1976); 1 UK (*Don't Go Breaking My Heart*)

The Dynamic Superiors

It was a long time coming – more than 10 years, in fact – but the Dynamic Superiors finally got their Motown contract in 1974. The quintet had been rehearsing together since their junior high school days in Washington, DC, and when they made it to the big stage some first-time observers gaped open-mouthed. The group were unusual for their time in that they made no secret of the fact that lead singer Tony Washington was gay. Indeed, Washington revelled in his sexuality, sometimes dressing in drag as the band went through their energetic and innovative choreographies. He wasn't the Dynamic Superiors' only gay member; the other preferred to stay anonymous, although Washington would sometimes tease audiences: 'I hope you don't think I'm the only one up here.' They were no Four Tops or Temptations, but the group recorded four albums for Motown – *The Dynamic Superiors* and *Pure Pleasure* (both 1975; both reached number 36 in the R&B Albums chart), *You Name It* (1976) and *Give And Take* (1977) – and achieved moderate success in the R&B and disco charts. *Shoe Shoe Shine* was a hit in 1974 and 1975's *Face The Music* proved a favourite of the disco crowd. The group made their last recording in 1980 but George Spann formed an act of the same name, featuring members of the Flamingos, in 2006.

Below: *The Dynamic Superiors – energetic, innovative choreography*

Founded: 1963
Origin: Washington, DC
Type: R&B, soul
Members: Michael McCalpin, George Peterback Jr, George Spann, Maurice Washington, Tony Washington
Highest chart positions: 68 US R&B (*Shoe Shoe Shine*, 1974); 13 US R&B (*Leave It Alone*, 1975)

Billy Eckstine

Below: *Billy Eckstine – huge influence on R&B vocalists*

The name of Billy Eckstine might be the last you would expect to see in a book on Motown stars. But the truth is the smooth-voiced jazzman had his pop moments, and he recorded three albums for Motown in the mid-60s that afforded him some of his highest chart placings. What's more, his soulful vocal style has been a big influence on R&B performers from Sam Cooke to Prince and many a Motown name. His first outing on the label came in 1965, when he released *The Prime Of My Life*, which peaked at number eight on the R&B album chart – his loftiest ever position – the following year. In 1966 came *My Way*, which did not achieve the same success, and 1968 saw the release of *For Love Of Ivy*, which penetrated the top 30 on the R&B chart and even the main Billboard 200. The best way now to appreciate his time at Motown is to buy *Billy Eckstine – The Motown Years*, released in 2004. It's a fine two-CD set showcasing the three albums and featuring a plethora of William 'Mickey' Stevenson-produced songs such as *The Prime Of My Life*, *As Long As She Needs Me* and *Time After Time* – even *Climb Every Mountain*. Some were also written by Stevenson, with Motown stalwarts like Stevie Wonder, Henry Cosby, Sylvia Moy and Harvey Fuqua among others with writing credits.

Born: 8 July 1914, Pittsburgh, Pennsylvania
Died: 8 March 1993, Pittsburgh, Pennsylvania
Type: jazz, pop
Highest chart positions: 76 US (*The Bitter With The Sweet*, 1956); 84 US R&B (*The Best Thing*, 1976)

Dennis Edwards

To join the Temptations might be considered the highlight of any singer's career. To join them three times, as Dennis Edwards did, is a feat quite out of the ordinary – but then Edwards is no ordinary vocalist. His singing career started out, as did those of so many Motown greats, in a gospel group in Detroit, and he then formed a soul/jazz band named Dennis Edwards & the Firebirds. That's where bass player James Jamerson, one of Motown's legendary session musicians, heard him and suggested he audition for Berry Gordy. Soon Edwards was recording with the Contours, but it was when he was called up to replace David Ruffin as the lead singer of the Temptations, in 1968, that he hit the big time. *Cloud Nine* and *Papa Was A Rolling Stone* were just a couple of the hits on which he starred. He left the Temps in 1997 only to rejoin in 1979 and leave again in 1983. Then came a solo career that featured the wonderful *Don't Look Any Further*, made in 1984 with Siedah Garrett, and *Coolin'*

Out (1985) before Edwards retraced his steps and joined the Temptations once again in 1987. There was a brief period in which he toured with former Temps Ruffin and Eddie Kendricks, but nowadays he harks back to golden days with the Temptations Review featuring Dennis Edwards.

Above: *Dennis Edwards – once, twice, three times a Temptation*

Born: 3 February 1943, Fairfield, Alabama
Type: R&B, soul, pop, disco
Highest chart position as a solo artist: 2 US (*Don't Look Any Further* with Siedah Garrett, 1984)

The Elgins

THE ELGINS

Right: *The Elgins – their Heaven Must Have Sent You found favour with British audiences second time around*

Johnny Dawson, Robert Fleming, Norbert McClean and Cleo 'Duke' Miller had already been singing together, under such varied guises as the Five Emeralds, the Sensations and the Downbeats, when they first recorded for Motown in 1962. Label boss Berry Gordy advised that they add female singer Saundra Mallett (later Edwards) to their number, and that they change their name from the Downbeats to the Elgins (a name that had already been used by the Temptations) when their first single, *Darling Baby*, came out in 1965. What Mr Gordy wanted, Mr Gordy invariably got. Both A-side and B-side (*Put Yourself In My Place*) made the pop charts, but they were overhauled by *Heaven Must Have Sent You*, released in July 1966 in the States and November in the UK. First time around, British audiences gave the record the thumbs-down, but when it was re-released five years later it soared to number three in the charts and has been fondly remembered ever since. Sadly, the definitive version of the Elgins did not survive the failure of the follow-up *I Understand My Man*, and broke up in 1967, although other versions have toured since then.

Founded: 1962
Origin: Detroit, Michigan
Type: R&B, soul, pop
Members: Yvonne Vernee Allen, Jimmy Charles, Johnny Dawson, William Devase, Saundra Mallett Edwards, Robert Fleming, Barbara Lewis, Darryl Lewis, Norbert McClean, Oscar McDonald, Cleo Miller, Kenny Sinclair, Jimmy Smith
Highest chart positions: 72 US, 4 US R&B (*Darling Baby*, 1965); 3 UK (*Heaven Must Have Sent You*, 1971)

Yvonne Fair

It found latter-day fame in Britain when it was featured in an episode of *The Vicar Of Dibley*, but that was not the only time *It Should Have Been Me* has appealed to the British. First given outings by Kim Weston and Gladys Knight, the strident plea for justice was subsequently a hit for Flora Yvonne Coleman, better known as Yvonne Fair, in 1976. Perhaps Fair had a previous episode in her career in mind when she put a megaton of feeling into her interpretation of the song: while she was working as part of the James Brown Revue she had recorded the song *I Found You*, which the boss later appropriated for his own use in the guise of the soul monster *I Got You (I Feel Good)*. Fair had already been part of a version of the Chantels before she got the Brown gig, and having been round the block with the Godfather of Soul and worked with singer Chuck Jackson, she signed to Motown in the early 70s. A part in the movie *Lady Sings The Blues* followed, and then she fell to working with producer Norman Whitfield on developing her raucous,

funky sound. *Funky Music Sho Nuff Turns Me On* declared a 1974 single, and it duly proceeded to turn on generations of fans.

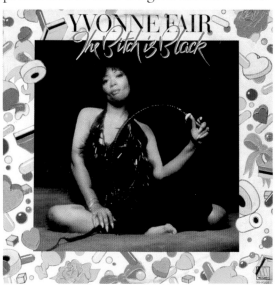

Left: *Yvonne Fair – funky music sho nuff turned her on*

Born: 21 October 1942, Richmond, Virginia
Died: 6 March 1994, Las Vegas, Nevada
Type: R&B, soul
Highest chart positions: 85 US (*It Should Have Been Me*, 1976); 32 US R&B (*Funky Music Sho Nuff Turns Me On*, 1974); 5 UK (*It Should Have Been Me*)

The Fantastic Four

Wallace 'Toby' Childs, 'Sweet' James Epps and Joseph and Ralph Pruitt, the founding members of the Fantastic Four, are not be confused with the comic book superheroes of the same name. These guys were R&B through and through, and they were originally the stars of the Ric-Tic label, outselling even the venerable Edwin Starr. Childs and Ralph Pruitt were replaced by Cleveland Horne and Ernest Newsome, and the group's first Ric-Tic hits were *The Whole World Is A Stage* and *You Gave Me Something (And Everything's Alright)*. When Motown bought Ric-Tic it was buying a group in form – an impression given substance when *I Love You Madly* reached number 12 on the R&B chart in 1968. The Fantastic Four came to the fore once again during the age of disco, releasing moderately successful singles on the Westbound label, and they kept on working as times and fashions changed. In 1990 they recorded *Working On A Building Of Love* for the British Motorcity label – set up by producer Ian Levine to showcase material by former Motown artists – but the group suffered an irreversible setback with the deaths of Horne and Epps in 2000.

THE FANTASTIC FOUR

HAVE A BRAND NEW SINGLE TO FOLLOW THEIR FIRST BLOCKBUSTER **"THE WHOLE WORLD IS A STAGE"**

Out a week and on the Charts heading for the Top!
BILLBOARD 87 *

YOU GAVE ME SOMETHING
(AND EVERYTHING IS ALL RIGHT)
Ric-Tic 128

THE FANTASTIC FOUR

RIC-TIC RECORDS

2307 Edison
Detroit, Michigan
(313) TO 9-2336   Exclusive Booking: **Q**BC

Founded: 1965
Origin: Detroit, Michigan
Type: R&B, soul, pop
Members: Wallace Childs, James Epps, Cleveland Horne, Ernest Newsome, Joseph Pruitt, Ralph Pruitt
Highest chart positions: 55 US (*You Gave Me Something (And Everything's Alright)*, 1967); 6 US R&B (*The Whole World Is A Stage*, 1967)

The Four Tops

The Four Tops were perhaps the archetypal Motown group. They had periods away from the label but they exemplified its spirit and style; they were as long-lived as any group can expect to be; they went four decades, without a single change in personnel, in challenging the Temptations and the Supremes as the label's premier forgers of hit sounds. In a way, the Four Tops *were* Holland-Dozier-Holland and they *were* Motown, their name springing readily to mind when you think of the Detroit sound, with Levi Stubbs' deep, pleading voice forcing itself to the forefront of your consciousness. The group got together as far back as 1953, when Stubbs, Abdul 'Duke' Fakir, Renaldo 'Obie' Benson and Lawrence Payton met and sang for the first time at a friend's birthday party. Styling themselves the Four Aims, they won an audition for the Chess label with the help of Payton's cousin Roquel Davis (who would go on to form a songwriting partnership with Berry Gordy). Chess signed the group and, changing their name to the Four Tops, they released records that went nowhere. There were similar stories when the group worked stints at Red Top, Riverside, and Columbia, but in 1963 came the switch that would make them: Gordy was by now a long-term friend, and a move to his company seemed inevitable at some stage. After a brief flirtation with Gordy's jazz-oriented Workshop label, the Tops were united with the Holland-Dozier-Holland team and found their natural home. The hits were not long in coming. *Baby I Need Your Loving* (1964) was followed by *Ask The Lonely* (1965) and then, in the same year, the group's US first chart-topper: *I Can't Help Myself (Sugar Pie,*

Honey Bunch). Britain was also taking the Four Tops to its heart, and after *I Can't Help Myself*, *It's The Same Old Song* and *Loving You Is Sweeter Than Ever* had made the top 30, *Reach Out I'll Be There* went all the way in 1966. It was a huge hit throughout the world, the second Motown number one in Britain (after the Supremes' *Baby Love* in 1964) and it became the Tops' signature tune. Nothing after that could top the success of *Reach Out* – although *Standing In The Shadows Of Love* (1966) and *Bernadette* (1967) ran it close – but that's not to say the Four Tops were finished with the business of making hits. Far from it: they carried on making the charts until 1983. But with Holland-Dozier-Holland's departure from Motown in 1967 the magic levels had dipped somewhat, and

when the label moved its HQ to Los Angeles in 1972 it heralded the parting of the ways for group and label. They reunited in 1983, and in 1997 the original foursome was broken up by Payton's death. The kings were dead; long live the kings.

Founded: 1953
Origin: Detroit, Michigan
Type: R&B, soul, doo-wop, pop, jazz
Members: Renaldo Benson, Harold Bonhart, Abdul Fakir, Ronnie McNeir, Lawrence Payton, Theo Peoples, Levi Stubbs
Highest chart positions: 1 US, 1 US R&B (*I Can't Help Myself (Sugar Pie, Honey Bunch)*, 1965, *Reach Out I'll Be There*, 1966); 1 UK (*Reach Out I'll Be There*)

The Funk Brothers

Session musicians are special people, giving freely of their talents, sometimes for small returns, often knowing full well their names might never go further than the limits of the studio. The loose assembly of session men known collectively as the Funk Brothers were *really* special people. Theirs was not to reason why; theirs was but to funk and fly. Operating at the time under strict anonymity, they provided the musical backing for so many Motown records from the late 1950s until 1972 that it's almost impossible to count them. They were the creators of the Motown sound, the smooth yet exciting R&B that sold Detroit to the world, yet they never received a hundredth of the credit accorded to the stars who warbled, growled and crooned in front of them. These brilliant musicians were signed to exclusive contracts that restricted their work outside the confines of the Motown studios, although some managed to indulge in a little moonlighting. It's only in recent years, with the publication of

the book *Standing In The Shadows Of Motown* and the distribution of a documentary of the same name, that a little light has been shed on these studio geniuses. The first Funk Brothers assembled when Berry Gordy scoured the clubs of Detroit for experienced and exceptionally able blues, jazz and R&B musicians in 1959. That was when

Above: *Funk Brother Eddie 'Chank' Willis – played on hundreds of hits*

the legendary bassist James Jamerson (the subject of the book mentioned above) began to get together with the likes of pianists Joe Hunter and Earl Van Dyke, drummers 'Benny' Benjamin and 'Pistol' Allen and guitarists Robert White, Eddie Willis and Joe Messina to craft the sounds Gordy was demanding. The Funk Brothers nickname came into existence as the camaraderie grew among the tightly drilled musicians.

Pop music masterpieces rolled off the production line in an hour or less as the Brothers got down to work, trading fraternal insults as they toiled. Sessions started at 10am and were finished by the afternoon, but Brothers could find themselves working seven days a week, being paid $10 a song for their efforts. As musical fashions changed, so did some of the musicians, with guitarist Wah Wah Watson coming to the fore as Norman Whitfield's psychedelia-tinged mini-symphonies found favour. And then suddenly, in 1972, it was over. Gordy moved the Motown operation to LA and the Funk Brothers were no more. The last masterwork on which the band of brothers collaborated was Marvin Gaye's 1971 album *What's Going On* – and what a record to remember them by.

Founded: 1959

Origin: Detroit, Michigan

Type: R&B, soul, funk

Members: among many others, Richard 'Pistol' Allen, Jack Ashford, Bob Babbitt, Marcus Belgrave, William 'Benny' Benjamin, Jack Brokensha, Eddie 'Bongo' Brown, Dennis Coffey, Henry 'Hank' Cosby, Marvin Gaye, Cornelius Grant, Johnny Griffith, Michael Henderson, Joe Hunter, James Jamerson, Uriel Jones, Joe Messina, Ray Monette, William 'Wild Bill' Moore, Ray Parker Jr, Melvin 'Wah Wah Watson' Ragin, Paul Riser, Marvin Tarplin, Earl Van Dyke, Freddie Waits, Robert White, Eddie 'Chank' Willis, Richard 'Popcorn' Wylie

Highest chart positions: just about any Motown number one between 1959 and 1972

Marvin Gaye

No one illustrates the rise of rhythm and blues from its simple foundations to the sophisticated levels of today better than Marvin Pentz Gaye Jr. This was a man of genius whose career stretched from doo-wop beginnings in the 50s to the 80s, when he led the way with his commentaries on social and sexual politics. In between, he helped to shape the Motown sound with a seemingly endless string of hits, on his own or in collaboration with other artists but always endeavouring to stretch the boundaries. The dream ended when his father shot him dead during an argument in 1984, but Gaye's music and heritage live on. His father was a preacher, and it was in his church that Gaye had started to sing, adding organ and drums to his skills as he grew. Soon he was involved in street-corner doo-wop groups and forming his own, named the Marquees. In 1958, Harvey Fuqua hired the group to act as his backing band, the Moonglows, and Fuqua's girlfriend, Gwen Gordy, introduced Gaye to her brother Berry at a party in 1960. It was to be a family affair: Gaye married Anna Gordy, Berry's other sister whom he had met at that party, in 1964. Back at work, however, it wasn't long before he had signed to the Motown subsidiary label Tamla, although his first engagements were humble: as a session drummer he played on all the early hits of Smokey Robinson & the Miracles. His fourth single as a singer, *Stubborn Kind Of Fellow* (1962), provided his first success, reaching number eight on the R&B chart, and it unleashed a torrent

Above: : *Marvin Gaye – made some of the most acclaimed popular music ever*

It On (1973) was described as one of the most sexually charged albums ever recorded. By the end of the 70s Gaye was suffering from drug and tax problems, and he left Motown in 1982. It's tragic to relate that from there it was mostly downhill, with Gaye suffering from depression and a deteriorating relationship with his father, and threatening suicide. His father's gun ensured he never had to carry out the threat.

of hits that would take him into the 70s and beyond. Switching styles from mid-tempo ballad to more energetic dance numbers as regularly as he changed producers (Holland-Dozier-Holland, Norman Whitfield, Smokey Robinson) and singing partners (Mary Wells, Kim Weston, Tammi Terrell, Diana Ross), Gaye just couldn't keep out of the charts. *How Sweet It Is (To Be Loved By You)* provided his first top ten entry, although his first number one didn't arrive until 1968 – but what a groundbreaking record *I Heard It Through The Grapevine* was. Gaye's music underwent a dramatic change as the 70s dawned and he gained complete artistic control over his music. The *What's Going On* song cycle, released in album form in 1971, confirmed his desire to comment on what he saw happening around him, while *Let's Get*

Born: 12 April 1939, Washington, DC
Died: 1 April 1984, Los Angeles, California
Type: R&B, soul, funk
Highest chart positions: 1 US, 1 US R&B (*I Heard It Through The Grapevine*, 1968, *Let's Get It On*, 1973, *Got To Give It Up*, 1977); 1 US R&B (*I'll Be Doggone* and *Ain't That Peculiar*, both 1965, *Ain't Nothing Like The Real Thing* and *You're All I Need To Get By*, both with Tammi Terrell, both 1968, *Too Busy Thinking About My Baby*, 1969, *What's Going On*, *Mercy Mercy Me (The Ecology)* and *Inner City Blues (Make Me Wanna Holler)*, all 1971, *I Want You*, 1976, *Sexual Healing*, 1982); 1 UK (*I Heard It Through The Grapevine*)

Johnny Gill

Johnny Gill's beginnings in the music game came when he was a kid in a gospel group called Wings of Faith. He has gone on to star as a member of New Edition since 1987 as well as carving out a celestial career as a supplier of solo and duet hits aplenty. His first recordings were for the Cotillion label, starting in 1983, but Gill's solo star began to rise when he released his first Motown album, simply titled *Johnny Gill*, in 1990 (by then he'd already replaced Bobby Brown in New Edition). Containing the number three single *Rub You The Right Way*, the number 10 hit *My, My, My* and two further top 100 songs, the album peaked at eight in the Billboard 200 and made Gill's name as a solo artist. To follow that success, he made *Provocative* (1993), which relied largely on the songwriting team of James Harris III and Terry Lewis, went gold and yielded three more R&B hits: *The Floor, Long Way From Home* and *Quiet Time To Play. Let's Get The Mood Right*, which saw the light of day in 1996 and also yielded gold-rating

Left: *Johnny Gill – rub him the right way, and my, my, my …*

sales, was Gill's last album with Motown. *Love Songs*, a Motown compilation, was released in 2005. Love Songs, a Motown compilation, was released in 2005 and its formula was followed by the similar Ballads in 2013.

> **Born:** 22 May 1966, Washington, DC
> **Type:** R&B, soul, new jack swing, pop
> **Highest chart positions** as a solo artist: 3 US, 1 US R&B (*Rub You The Right Way*, 1990); 1 US R&B (*Where Do We Go From Here* with Stacy Lattisaw, 1989, *My, My, My*, 1990, *Wrap My Body Tight*, 1991); 17 UK (*Slow And Sexy* with Shabba Ranks, 1992)

The Good Girls

Motown had a vision for the Good Girls: they would be the Supremes of the 90s, updated with a contemporary urban sound and benefiting from the interest around Teddy Riley and Bernard Belle's new jack swing movement. The trio certainly looked the part and sounded good, breaking into the R&B charts on several occasions. But, if we're being honest, they never had a chance of emulating Diana Ross and Co; that was just too much to ask. In an era that also saw the promotion of Motown acts like Johnny Gill, the Boys, MC Trouble, Milira and Rich Nice, the Good Girls were launched with a fresh, funky album, *All For Your Love*, that included a remake of the 1966 Supremes song *Love Is Like An Itching In My Heart*. Also on the album was the single *My Sweetness*, which got the girls as high on the R&B chart as they would ever go. In 1990 the group set off on two tours that saw their popularity peak – Motown's MotorTown tour and, later, New Kids on the Block's No More Games trek. Two years later came the second album, *Just Call Me*, and it served up a hit in the form of the title track. Around the same time, the group were supplying backing vocals for rapper YoYo's album *Black Pearl*. After that, they sank into the background.

Founded: 1989
Origin: Los Angeles, California
Type: R&B, soul, new jack swing
Members: Shireen Crutchfield, DeMonica Santiago, Joyce Tolbert
Highest chart position: 6 US R&B (*Your Sweetness*, 1990)

Herman Griffin

Herman Griffin never made the charts, which is more than a little ironic considering he worked in the promotions department at Motown. He earns his place in this book because of the important role he played in the very beginnings of the Motown empire: he became the performer of the first song ever published under Berry Gordy's Jobete publishing company when he recorded *I Need You* for HOB Records. The name Jobete came from the first two letters of Berry's children's names – Joy, Berry and Terry – while HOB had its source in the House of Beauty, a hairdressing salon patronised by Gordy's future wife Raynoma Liles. The recording of *I Need You* also saw the first credited performance of the Rayber Voices, the backing singers (including Raynoma and Brian Holland) who were used in early Motown sessions before the advent of the Andantes. Gordy had seen Griffin in action at a club and marvelled at his acrobatic performance in which back-flips, somersaults and splits vied with his tenor voice for attention. Gordy's first attempt at selling him to the public fell on deaf ears, however. So did the next one, *True Love*, which was released on Tamla Records in October 1960, and the next, *Sleep (Little One)* (Motown, 1962). It seemed that, deprived of the acrobatics, Griffin offered too little as a selling proposition. He had the connections, being married to Mary Wells for a while (and allegedly easing her exit from Motown), but it just didn't work.

Born: November 1936, Selma, Alabama
Died: November 1989
Type: R&B

Sam Harris

Sam Harris moved to Los Angeles in order to further his education at UCLA, but it was there that he also got his start in show business. Trying his luck in the first season of the TV talent show *Star Search* in 1984, he wound up as the champion with his rendition of *Over The Rainbow* and found himself the object of record companies' attention. So it was that he signed up with Motown and released his first album in the year of his TV triumph. *Sam Harris* included songs by the venerable likes of Rita Coolidge and Bruce Roberts, was greeted reasonably warmly by the critics and also found willing buyers, many of whom had no doubt been avid *Star Search* viewers. The album achieved gold status and reached number 35 on the album charts, while a single, *Sugar Don't Bite*, touched number 36 in the Billboard Hot 100. His next album, rejoicing in the corny title of *Sam-I-Am* (1985) and featuring songwriting and production credits for Harris, did not do so well, although the single *I'd*

Do It All Again almost broke into the top 50. But it was not all about making records for Harris, who went on to show his versatility through his work on Broadway, in concert at venues as diverse as the White House and New York's Carnegie Hall and in writing and producing TV shows including *Down To Earth*.

Born: 4 June 1961, Cushing, Oklahoma
Type: R&B, pop, rock
Highest chart position: 36 US (*Sugar Don't Bite*, 1984)

High Inergy

Discovered by Gwen Gordy Fuqua – one of the most distinguished of the Gordy clan, who wrote songs and married Harvey Fuqua alongside helping to run the Motown business – High Inergy were a quartet who clinched a record deal in 1977. The Mitchell sisters Vernessa and Barbara provided a striking vocal presence while Linda Howard and Michelle Martin (known as Rumph) focused primarily on dancing, and the girls modelled themselves on the Supremes and the Vandellas. Their first album, *Turnin' On*, released the same year, zoomed high into the charts and yielded the single *You Can't Turn Me Off (In The Middle of Turning Me On)*, an atmospheric ballad that had a chart life of its own. *Steppin' Out* was the next album, released the following year, and it also charted and yielded a single, *Love Is All You Need*, that penetrated the Hot 100. But that was the last time High Inergy were to achieve top 50 status. Lead singer Vernessa Mitchell left to follow a successful career in gospel music and

her duties were taken over by her sister Barbara. It wasn't quite the same as a trio, and the group broke up in 1984 to follow solo careers after scoring a total of nine R&B hits. Linda Howard died in 2012.

Above: *High Inergy – modelled themselves on the Supremes and the Vandellas*

Founded: 1977
Origin: Pasadena, California
Type: R&B, soul, pop, disco
Members: Linda Howard, Michelle Martin, Barbara Mitchell, Vernessa Mitchell
Highest chart positions: 12 US, 2 US R&B (*You Can't Turn Me Off (In The Middle Of Turning Me On)*, 1977)

Holland-Dozier-Holland

With Holland-Dozier-Holland, Motown had the complete package required to take their stable of stars, arrange and rearrange them around the songs they wrote, instil the Motown sound in the recordings they made and give them sure-fire hits. This was a dream songwriting and production team, a goose that laid clutches of golden eggs and came up with records that would be hummed and played on a million radios decades after they were made. It's quite impossible to envisage a time when the likes of *Baby Love, Reach Out I'll Be There* or *Where Did Our Love Go* won't be popular. Yet it all started out of a kind of adversity: the looming inevitability of the failure of Eddie Holland's singing career. Eddie had been working with Berry Gordy since before the latter had even

formed the label (Gordy had produced Eddie's 1958 single on Mercury, *You*) and had had a career of sorts under the Motown imprint. His only top 30 hit, *Jamie*, came in 1961, however, and Gordy decided to team him up with brother Brian, a staff songwriter who had co-written *Please Mr Postman* for the Marvelettes, and Lamont Dozier, who had recorded for the Motown subsidiary Mel-o-dy. It was a match made in heaven. The trio found that writing and producing – Dozier and Brian would compose the music and oversee the studio production while Eddie would write the lyrics and arrange the vocals – were preferable to performing, and they were away. Over the next five or six years they would create and preside over the birth of no fewer than 25 number one hit singles, with most kudos coming their way for their work with the Four Tops and the Supremes. A quick glance over the following list of hits will convince any doubters of the quality of Holland-Dozier-Holland's work: *Where*

Did Our Love Go, Baby Love, Come See About Me, Back In My Arms Again, I Hear A Symphony, You Can't Hurry Love, You Keep Me Hangin' On, Love Is Here And Now You're Gone, The Happening (all for the Supremes); *I Can't Help Myself (Sugar Pie Honey Bunch), Reach Out I'll Be There, Bernadette* (for the Four Tops); *(Love Is Like A) Heatwave, Nowhere To Run, I'm Ready For Love, Jimmy Mack* (all for Martha Reeves & the Vandellas); *How Sweet It Is (To Be Loved By You)* for Marvin Gaye. All good things come to an end as they say, and by 1967 Holland-Dozier-Holland were airing a grudge with Gordy over the issues of profit-sharing and royalties. The matter escalated until the trio became sufficiently aggrieved to leave Motown and try their luck elsewhere. It was the label's loss, for the H-D-H hits didn't stop: *Give Me Just A Little More Time* by Chairmen of the Board and Freda Payne's *Band Of Gold* were just a couple of their post-Motown hits.

Founded: 1962

Origin: Detroit, Michigan

Type: R&B, soul

Members: Lamont Dozier, Brian Holland, Eddie Holland

Highest chart positions: many hits from acts such as the Supremes, the Four Tops, Martha & the Vandellas, Junior Walker & the All-Stars, the Isley Brothers and the Elgins between 1962 and 1968

Brenda Holloway

Growing up in the Watts neighbourhood of Los Angeles, Brenda Holloway took naturally to music, learning violin and singing in church with her sister Patrice. She first entered a recording studio at the age of 14, and soon she and Patrice were getting session work as singers. Brenda was spotted by Berry Gordy at a convention in LA, where she sang the Mary Wells hit *My Guy*, and, impressed by her powerful, ballsy vocals, Gordy signed her to the Tamla label. Holloway almost immediately struck pay dirt with her first single, *Every Little Bit Hurts*. Gordy was not the only one impressed by her performances: the hit song became a favourite of British R&B groups, and she found herself opening for the Beatles on their 1965 US tour. Holloway continued to frequent the charts with songs like *I'll Always Love You* and *When I'm Gone*, but relations with Motown were starting to sour, and matters came to a head when Gordy binned her second album. Holloway, who felt she was being given second-rate material, started writing songs with Patrice – *You've Made Me So Very Happy* would turn out to be a hit for the jazz-rock band Blood Sweat & Tears. The second album was finally released in 1968, but by that time Holloway was turning her back on the music industry, to which she did not return until 1980.

Born: 21 June 1946, Atascadero, California
Type: R&B, soul
Highest chart positions: 13 US (*Every Little Bit Hurts*, 1964), 12 US R&B (*When I'm Gone*, 1965)

Thelma Houston

If ever a singer put her own stamp on a song that had already been a success for another act, it was when Thelma Houston reinterpreted *Don't Leave Me This Way*, a hit for Harold Melvin & the Bluenotes in 1975. The following year, the Grammy judges were so impressed by Houston's vocal bravura that they awarded her Best Female R&B Vocal Performance, and rightly so. The Gamble/Huff song had originally been earmarked as Diana Ross's follow-up to *Love Hangover*, but we can be grateful that Motown changed their minds, and that Houston (no relation to Whitney) changed the direction of her career from healthcare to music. Originally recording for Dunhill, she hit the charts in 1970 with Laura Nyro's *Save The Country* before switching to Motown's MoWest label. Issuing a good few singles without great success, she also appeared in the 1976 Motown baseball film *The Bingo Long Traveling All Stars And Motor Kings* and appeared on Jermaine Jackson's hit album *My Name Is Jermaine*. Then came the release of Houston's *Any Way You Like It* album (1976), containing the track that made her and inspired artists such as the Communards to try to do better (they failed). There were other hits, *If It's The Last Thing I Do* and *Saturday Night, Sunday Morning* among them, but the name of Thelma Houston will always be associated with one song.

Left: *Thelma Houston – took a song intended for Diana Ross and made it her own*

Born: 7 May 1946, Leland, Mississippi
Type: soul, R&B, disco, gospel
Highest chart positions: 1 US, 1 US R&B (*Don't Leave Me This Way*, 1976); 13 UK (*Don't Leave Me This Way*, 1977)

Willie Hutch

Born in California but brought up in Texas, William Hutchinson abbreviated his name when his doo-wop talents were noted and he was picked up by the Soul City label. Back once again in LA, he began writing, arranging and producing for the vocal group the 5th Dimension and then, after being signed by RCA, he released two albums. It was at this point that Hal Davis, needing lyrics for a piece he'd written for the Jackson 5, called Hutch and asked him to oblige. The Jacksons recorded *I'll Be There* the next morning. That was sufficient evidence for Berry Gordy that here was a talent he needed on his side, and soon Hutch was working as a songwriter, arranger, producer and musician at Motown. His name appeared on records by Marvin Gaye, the Miracles, Michael Jackson and Smokey Robinson and, from 1973, Hutch started making regular appearances in the R&B charts on his own account. That year he unveiled his *Fully Exposed* album and provided the soundtrack for the blaxploitation film *The Mack*, and two years later he was attaining his highest ever spot on the R&B chart with the single *Love Power*. He spent five years away from Motown but went back in 1982 to make the song that would be his biggest British hit, *In And Out*.

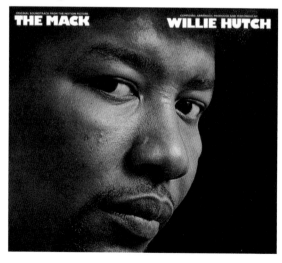

Born: 6 December 1944, Los Angeles, California
Died: 19 September 2005, Dallas, Texas
Type: R&B, soul, funk
Highest chart positions: 41 US, 8 US R&B (*Love Power*, 1975); 51 UK (*In And Out,* 1982)

India.Arie

Her parents were from Memphis and Detroit, so it was always likely that India Arie Simpson would have R&B and soul coursing through her veins. So it has proved, and now India.Arie is the proud possessor of three Grammy Awards and the creator of records that have sold more than 10 million copies around the world. With her roots firmly in the work of past Motown and other R&B and soul artists, she's nevertheless able to bring her own 21st century style to the table, as songwriter, musician, singer and producer. India spent her teenage years in Atlanta, Georgia, where she discovered in herself a rare songwriting talent, and in 1999 she opted in to a record deal with Universal/Motown. Her debut album, *Acoustic Soul*, was released to a delighted world in 2001 and went double platinum in America. *Voyage To India* followed in 2002 and went higher in the charts, hitting the number six spot on the Billboard 200 and earning its creator two Grammies. A natural progression seemed to be developing and, sure enough, album number three, *Testimony: Vol 1, Life & Relationship*, soared to the top of the album chart and provided a hit single in *I Am Not My Hair*, featuring Akon. India's *Testimony: Vol 2, Life & Politics* (2009) made it to third position in the chart and this extraordinary musician's 2013 album *Songversation* peaked at number seven.

Left: *India.Arie – a rare songwriting and performing talent*

Born: 3 October 1975, Denver, Colorado
Type: R&B, soul, neo soul
Highest chart positions: 47 US, 14 R&B (*Video*, 2001); 29 UK (*Brown Skin*, 2001)

The Isley Brothers

They came, they saw, they conquered, they lived through a thousand sea changes in musical fashion and, finally, they petered out. And through it all, as generation succeeded generation, the Isley Brothers came up with some of the most classy, infectious popular music there's ever been, influencing countless other artists along the way. The first generation of brothers came out of Ohio, where they had been schooled in music by a father who was himself a professional singer. They were a gospel quartet at first, with Ronald succeeding Vernon (who died in 1955) as the lead singer, but when they went to New York in 1957 it was to record some doo-wop singles. They first really came to notice when a song based around their catchphrase 'you know you make me want to shout' hit the top 50 in 1957; *Shout* has been covered many times since, notably by Lulu in the

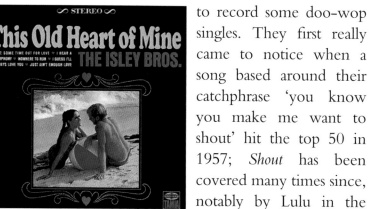

UK. *Twist And Shout* (1962) was another fan pleaser, reaching number 17 in the US and 42 in Britain, but there were more misses than hits as they went through a plethora of record deals, giving a job to a young guitarist named James Marshall Hendrix along the way. That is until Motown took the brothers under its wing in 1965 and put them on its Tamla label. Britain just loved *This Old Heart Of Mine (Is Weak For You)*, released the following year, and the US was pretty impressed too; the Holland-Dozier-Holland production took the Isleys all the way to 12th place on the Billboard Hot 100. The Tamla years produced loved songs like *I Guess I'll Always Have You* and *Behind A Painted Smile*, the latter proving a massive hit in Britain but, strangely, less popular in the US. Recognising the Brits' excellent taste in music, the Isleys moved to the UK in 1967, taking in all that was happening as England swung like a pendulum do. In truth, the band, seasoned songwriters and musicians, felt constrained by the strict Motown

production model, and by the time they returned to America in 1969 they had left Tamla for the more comforting confines of their own T-Neck label. That it was a good move was proved by the success of their next single, *It's Your Thing*, which made number two in the US charts while merely hitting 30 in Britain. By this time new, younger Isleys including brother-in-law Chris Jasper were coming through, and the band's style was becoming rockier and more experimental. *That Lady* was a big hit in 1973, *Fight The Power* a slightly smaller one in 1975. There was another burst of hits in the 90s, but by 2006 illness and misfortune had combined to bring to an end one of the lengthiest and most pleasing of musical careers.

Founded: 1954

Origin: Cincinnati, Ohio

Type: R&B, rock 'n' roll, soul, doo-wop, funk, rock, gospel

Members: Ernie Isley, Marvin Isley, O'Kelly Isley, Ronald Isley, Rudolph Isley, Vernon Isley, Chris Jasper

Highest chart positions: 2 US, 1 US R&B (*It's Your Thing*, 1969); 1 US R&B (*Fight The Power (Part 1)*, 1977, *The Pride (Part 1)*, 1977, *Take Me To The Next Phase (Part 1)*, 1978, *I Wanna Be With You (Part 1)*, 1979, *Don't Say Goodnight (It's Time For Love) (Parts 1 & 2)*, 1980, *Down Low (Nobody Has To Know)* as R Kelly featuring the Isley Brothers, 1996); 3 UK (*This Old Heart Of Mine (Is Weak For You)*, 1966)

The Jackson 5

Below & Far Right: *The Jackson 5 – built a bridge between the innocent 1960s and the more worldly-wise 1970s*

Not only were the Jackson 5 significant for Motown in terms of the numbers of records they sold – and all told they have sold more than 100 million over the years – and the solo careers they launched, they were also the last of the classic groups to come out of the famous Detroit stable. Before the Jacksons' heyday in the early 1970s, Motown mostly meant the likes of the Temptations and the Four Tops, the Supremes and the Vandellas. As the Jacksons took the label smoothly into the new era, the Marvin Gayes and Stevie Wonders of this world were readying themselves to take Motown, and popular music in general, to new horizons. The Jackson 5 formed, if you like, a kind of bridge between the innocent 60s and the more worldly-wise 70s. The original band consisted of, in order of seniority, Jackie, Tito, Jermaine, Marlon and Michael, the sons of a strict Jehovah's Witness mother and an unpredictable, music-loving father. The latter had the idea of putting together some kind of family band and encouraged the three older sons to form a five-piece with two cousins. The cousins were replaced by Marlon and Michael as the group developed rapidly as musicians and performers, so it was no surprise when they won a talent contest at the legendary Apollo Theater in Harlem. At the Apollo that night was new fan Gladys Knight, who recommended the group to Motown. Berry Gordy signed the boys in 1968 and set about grooming them for stardom. The newly formed Corporation – Freddie Perren, Fonce Mizell and Deke Richards, replacements for the Holland-Dozier-Holland songwriting/production team – was tasked with coming up with

the group's material. The debut album, *Diana Ross Presents The Jackson 5,* came out in August 1969, the first single, *I Want You Back,* two months later and the game was afoot. The single rocketed to number one on the Billboard chart, as did the next three: *ABC, The Love You Save* and *I'll Be There,* which became Motown's biggest ever seller. Gordy had the label-saving new blood he needed. What's more, the Jacksons appealed to a wider audience than any of his previous artists, and the merchandising business flourished. Two number two singles, *Mama's Pearl* and *Never Can Say Goodbye* followed and by late 1971 the Jacksons were deemed sufficiently mature to issue a greatest hits album. The hits, although not reaching the peak of the first four singles, kept coming, and by the time the Jackson 5 left Motown for CBS in 1975 the legend was fully formed – and a couple of solo careers, those of Jermaine and Michael, had been launched to worldwide acclaim. There was much, much more to come from the Jacksons.

Founded: 1964

Origin: Gary, Indiana

Type: R&B, soul, pop, rock

Members: Jackie Jackson, Jermaine Jackson, Marlon Jackson, Michael Jackson, Randy Jackson, Tito Jackson

Highest chart positions: 1 US, 1 US R&B (*I Want You Back,* 1969, *ABC,* 1970, *The Love You Save,* 1970, *I'll Be There,* 1970); 1 US R&B (*Never Can Say Goodbye,* 1971, *Dancing Machine,* 1974); 1 UK (*Show You The Way To Go,* 1977)

Chuck Jackson

With his classy baritone soul voice and elegant interpretation of Burt Bacharach/Hal David numbers, Chuck Jackson (no relation to the Gary, Indiana family) made regular visits to the R&B charts in the 1960s, and even as late as 1973. His time at Motown, between 1967 and 1970, brought his fans such largely forgotten songs as *(You Can't Let The Boy In You Overpower) The Man In You, Are You Lonely For Me Baby* and *Honey Come Back* and, although he never hit the mainstream charts in the UK, he is a favourite of the Northern Soul crowd. He had a spell in the late 1950s with one of the most highly regarded doo-wop groups, the Dell-Vikings, but it was while he was singing in Jackie Wilson's Revue that he was picked up by Scepter Records in 1961. As well as the Bacharach/David material he recorded with the label, he worked with Lieber-Stoller songs (*I Keep Forgettin'*, 1962) and had some successful duets with Maxine Brown. Smokey Robinson was a prime influence in getting Jackson to move across to Motown, and there he recorded three albums: *Chuck Jackson Arrives, Goin' Back To Chuck Jackson* and *Teardrops Keep Falling On My Heart*. Two singles released on Tamla-Motown in the UK, *Girls Girls Girls* and *Honey Come Back*, remain close to the heart of collectors of rare grooves. Jackson continues to work to this day.

Born: 22 July 1937, Latta, South Carolina
Type: R&B, pop
Highest chart positions: 23 US, 2 US R&B (*Any Day Now (My Wild Beautiful Bird)*, 1962)

Jermaine Jackson

Jermaine Jackson had a special reason for staying loyal to Motown when his brothers left for CBS in 1975: he was married to one of Berry Gordy's daughters, Hazel. The relationship with the label lasted until 1983, when he upped sticks for Arista, and during that time he came up with regular R&B and mainstream chart hits. The fourth child of Katherine and Joe Jackson, Jermaine took on the lead vocal and rhythm guitar duties in the original family band, the Jackson Brothers, and remains known for his high-quality musicianship, no matter what genre he operates in. He's also adept at bass guitar and keyboards. With the Jackson 5 he was joint lead singer with Michael and featured prominently on hits like *I Want You Back* and *I'll Be There*. While still a band member he made the US top 10 with a cover version of *Daddy's Home*, but the Jacksons' split with Motown also signalled his departure from the group. A real highlight of his solo career was his 1980 Stevie Wonder-produced album *Let's Get Serious*, which

made number six on the Billboard 200 and earned Jermaine a Grammy nomination for Best Male R&B Vocal Performance. Wonder guested on vocals on the title track, which breached the top 10.

Left: *Jermaine Jackson – relationship with Motown by marriage*

Born: 11 December 1954, Gary, Indiana
Type: R&B, soul, funk, dance
Highest chart positions: 9 US, 1 US R&B (*Let's Get Serious*, 1980); 9 US (*Daddy's Home*, 1973); 1 US R&B (*Don't Take It Personal*, 1989); 6 UK (*Do What You Do*, 1984)

Michael Jackson

The show business juggernaut that was Michael Jackson was born the moment his father Joe decided that his children could be the means by which they could escape the steel city of Gary, Indiana. Michael certainly managed to leave Gary behind, but whether one of history's most successful musicians and performers ever managed to escape the demons of his childhood is another matter. No matter how risqué his dance moves, no matter how adult the themes of his work, it seemed the child was always content to stay hidden within

the man. But we are not here to probe a megastar's psyche; instead we celebrate his achievements, which were bigger and more varied in nature than those of almost any other entertainer. They started when Michael joined his brothers in the family band in 1963 at the age of just five, showing himself to be a child genius. Combining an extraordinarily mature vocal talent with mastery of the Godfather James Brown's dance moves, Michael demonstrated that he was born to lead. When the Jackson 5 joined Motown in 1968 and released *I Want You Back*, he was only 11 yet already a seasoned performer. It wasn't long before the label bosses, realising along with everyone else with eyes to see that they had something amazing on their books, began to groom him for the inevitable solo career. His first single, *Got To Be There* (1971) made the top five and the next, *Rockin' Robin* (1972), went higher. After a slight hiccup with the next two releases, Michael hit the top with the sentimental *Ben*, which had been written for another wonder

kid, Donnie Osmond. Having made four albums for Motown, in 1976 he decamped for Epic along with most of his brothers, leaving Jermaine alone at Motown. His first solo album for his new label, *Off The Wall* (1979), and its four top 10 singles showed the world's listeners that a new Michael Jackson, with his own ideas and the creative wherewithal to bring them to fruition, was walking among them. Next came *Thriller* (1982), which would go on to become the world's best-selling album of all time with perhaps as many as 65 million copies sold. Michael was already a long way from Gary, Indiana although still only 24 years old. There was still a long way for him to go before he met his untimely death in his bed in the summer of 2009. And there is no telling how long the Michael Jackson legend will continue to proliferate.

Born: 29 August 1958, Gary, Indiana
Died: 25 June 2009, Los Angeles, California
Type: R&B, soul, pop, funk, dance, disco
Highest chart positions: 1 US, 1 US R&B (*Don't Stop 'Til You Get Enough*, 1979, *Rock With You*, 1979, *Billie Jean* and *Beat It*, both 1983, *The Way You Make Me Feel, I Just Can't Stop Loving You* with Siedah Garrett and *Bad*, all 1987, *Man In The Mirror*, 1988, *You Are Not Alone*, 1995); 1 US (*Ben*, 1972, *Say Say Say* with Paul McCartney, 1983, *Dirty Diana*, 1988, *Black Or White*, 1991); 1 US R&B (*The Girl Is Mine* with Paul McCartney, 1983, *Another Part Of Me*, 1988, *Remember The Time* and *In The Closet*, both 1992); 1 UK (*One Day In Your Life*, 1975, *Billie Jean, I Just Can't Stop Loving You, Black Or White, You Are Not Alone, Earth Song*, 1995, *Blood On The Dance Floor*, 1997)

Rick James

Below: *Rick James – took funk to the masses*

Without Rick James around, the urgent, chugging rhythms of funk's invitation to the dance might never have crossed over to the mainstream pop audience. James was an innovator whose music has shaped the work of many a modern-day star, and he also helped to show Motown how to follow a direction that reaped handsome rewards. After an early musical education with doo-wop and R&B bands in his home town, James absented himself from the US Navy and surfaced in Canada, where his band the Mynah Birds included a youthful Neil Young. He was found by the authorities recording at Motown in the 1960s and a one-year prison sentence was the result. That interval over, he resumed his musical career as a staff writer at Motown and then, in 1977, signed for the subsidiary Gordy Records as a recording artist. His first album, *Come Get It!* (1978) yielded his biggest hit single, *You And I*, and went double platinum. Subsequent years brought James multiple successes on the R&B charts and, meanwhile, he was working behind the scenes with artists including Smokey Robinson, the Temptations and Eddie Murphy. The *Street Songs* album (1981) revived Motown's declining fortunes with sales of more than three million. Unfortunately, drug addictions and ill health curtailed James's career and he died an early death.

> **Born:** 1 February 1948, Buffalo, New York
> **Died:** 6 August 2004, Burbank, California
> **Type:** R&B, soul, funk, pop
> **Highest chart positions:** 13 US, 1 US R&B (*You And I*, 1978); 1 US R&B (*Give It To Me Baby*, 1981, *Cold Blooded*, 1983, *Loosey's Rap* featuring Roxanne Shanté, 1988); 41 UK (*Big Time*, 1980)

Mable John

The blues singer Mable John can be proud to declare a few wonderful music history distinctions: as the first woman to be signed to Berry Gordy's Tamla label she set the standard for many to come; she could claim Little Willie John (*Need Your Love So Bad*) as a brother; and she performed at the last show the legendary Billie Holiday ever played in Detroit, weeks before her death. But John doesn't need to play on the achievements of others; she is an accomplished entertainer in her own right who as late as 2007 was appearing in the blues film *Honeydripper*. John moved with her family to Detroit when she was young and later worked at an insurance agency run by Bertha Gordy, the mother of Berry. Meeting up with Mrs Gordy at a later date, she was intrigued to hear that her son was looking for musicians to record his songs. John and Gordy began to work together, making their first recordings in 1959. Then, after earning a deal with Tamla, John released her first single, *Who Wouldn't Love A Man Like That?* Remarkably, the Supremes were recruited to act as her backing vocalists. Sad to relate, blues music wasn't doing the business for Gordy and she left Motown in 1962 and went to record for Stax, for whom she registered her biggest hit.

Left: *Mable John – the first woman to sign to the Tamla label*

Born: 3 November 1930, Bastrop, Louisiana
Type: blues, R&B, gospel
Highest chart positions: 95 US, 6 US R&B (*Your Good Thing (Is About To End)*, 1966)

Marv Johnson

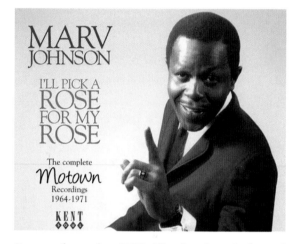

And the award for the first recording artist to appear on the label that would burgeon into the mighty Motown goes to … Marv Johnson. Actually it was on the Tamla Records label, and it had to be sold nationwide by United Artists because Tamla could only muster Detroit-wide distribution, but the record stands. Johnson had begun his musical career in a doo-wop group named the Serenaders, and Gordy had chanced upon the young singer, songwriter and pianist at a carnival. Into the studio went Johnson and out came the first Tamla single, *Come To Me* (written by Gordy and Johnson) in May 1959. And with the help of United Artists the record climbed as high as number 30 on the Hot 100. The songwriting partnership continued for another four songs, but Johnson was soon off to record for UA, with Gordy continuing as his manager. He hit the top 10 twice before returning in 1965 to Motown, where he joined the Gordy label and continued to pump out records. None of them succeeded in the States, but the UK liked what it heard from Johnson, buying *I'll Pick A Rose For My Rose* and *I Miss You Baby* (both 1969) in sufficient numbers to make them hits. Johnson later worked in promotions and as a writer for Motown, and carried on entertaining into the 1990s.

Born: 15 October 1938, Detroit, Michigan
Died: 16 May 1993, Columbia, South Carolina
Type: R&B, soul
Highest chart positions: 9 US, 2 US R&B (*I Love The Way You Love*, 1960); 7 UK (*You Got What It Takes*, 1960)

Kem

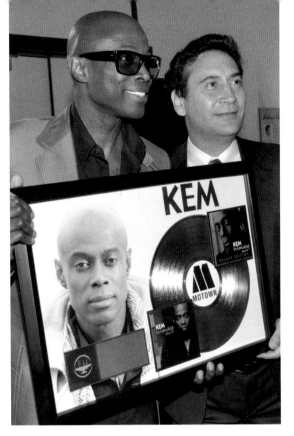

Born in Nashville but growing up in Detroit, Kim Owens encountered enough problems in his formative years to fuel a lifetime of songwriting, making music and producing records. And it was music, along with an exploration of his spirituality, that enabled the man who has become known as Kem to overcome estrangement from his family, homelessness and drug addiction. He has progressed to become one of the 21st century's most popular R&B artists, appealing to young and more mature listeners alike. The fact that he wrote, produced and self-released his first album, *Kemistry*, financing it with his credit card and wages from waiting tables and singing in a wedding band, shows how hard he was prepared to work to surmount his problems. Motown, recognising a good thing, came to the rescue by signing him in 2001 and re-released the album in 2003, watching as it went gold and made inroads into the top 100. As singles regularly adorned the R&B charts (*USA Today* described 2003's *Love Calls* as a Motown classic), further albums followed. They included *Album II*, which topped the R&B chart, made it to number five on the Billboard 200 and sold more than half a million copies across the USA. *Intimacy: Album III* (2010) performed even better, hitting number two in its first week and producing four R&B hit singles.

Born: 23 July 1969, Nashville, Tennessee
Type: R&B, soul, neo soul, jazz
Highest chart positions: 84 US (*I Can't Stop Loving You*, 2005); 17 US R&B (*Why Would You Stay*, 2010)

Eddie Kendricks

Some guys have all the luck. Eddie Kendricks was fortunate enough to have two hit-making careers, first as one of the stage-front singers with the Temptations, then as a major solo star all the way up to 1977. Active on the Alabama music scene with a group called the Primes, he moved to Detroit and was a major force in bringing the Temptations together in 1961. By the middle of the decade the group, with Kendricks' moving tenor and falsetto often prominent, had become massive stars with hits like *My Girl* and *Ain't Too Proud To Beg*. The year after he took the lead on *Just My Imagination*, he left the Temps to go solo – a move judged unwise by some but justified in view of the success he was about to experience. By 1973 he had hit the big time on both sides of the Atlantic with *Keep On Truckin'* and kept the pot boiling with *Boogie Down* (1974). Both of those songs came from highly acclaimed albums released on the Tamla label, and the relationship continued up to 1977's *Slick*, which yielded yet more R&B hits. Kendricks was only 52 years of age when he died of lung cancer back in his native Birmingham.

Born: 17 December 1939, Birmingham, Alabama
Died: 5 October 1992, Birmingham, Alabama
Type: R&B, soul, pop, disco
Highest chart positions: 1 US, 1 US R&B (*Keep On Truckin' (Part I)*, 1973); 1 US R&B (*Boogie Down*, 1974, *Shoeshine Boy*, 1975); 18 UK (*Keep on Truckin' (Part I)*)

Gladys Knight & The Pips

Motown has always been a family affair in one way and another, and Gladys Knight & the Pips were no exceptions. They came fully formed out of Atlanta, like many another R&B and soul act, in 1952: Gladys Knight (born 1944) with brother Merald (known to the world as Bubba), sister Brenda and cousins Eleanor and William Guest. There was little indication in those days that Gladys would one day be known as the Empress of Soul, but the Pips performed pleasingly enough and made their first recordings for Brunswick in 1958. Soon Brenda and Eleanor had left to get married, but there was a ready supply of cousins to take their places: Edward Patten and Langston George slipped seamlessly into the group. In 1961, *Every Beat Of My Heart*, on the Vee-Jay label, reached the Billboard top 10, but it wasn't until the

group moved over to Motown's Soul subsidiary and were teamed with writer/producer Norman Whitfield that the act now known as Gladys Knight & the Pips could be guaranteed to chart with every release. Although Gladys's bluesy vocals didn't quite fit the Motown model, there it was, in 1967, that they had a major hit with *I Heard It Through The Grapevine*, already recorded by Smokey Robinson & the Miracles and a year later covered in unforgettable style by Marvin Gaye. The Pips' version stayed at the top of the R&B chart for six weeks and narrowly missed top spot in the pop chart. Although Motown had regarded the group as a second-string act, the public begged to differ, and over the next six years a stream of hit singles followed. Among the highlights were *The End Of Our Road* (1968), *If I Were Your Woman*

Below: *Gladys Knight – stream of hits followed move to Motown*

Above: *Gladys Knight & the Pips – made their first recording in 1958*

(1970) and *Neither One Of Us (Wants To Be The First To Say Goodbye)* (1973). The last-named single was followed by the first failure for many a year, the Bacharach/David composition *The Look Of Love*, and shortly afterwards the group left for Buddah Records as Motown moved west to Hollywood. The winners didn't stop flowing, with *Midnight Train To Georgia* a sizeable hit in both US and UK and many others following. Gladys embarked on a solo career with the album *Miss Gladys Knight* in 1978, and chalked up a chart-topper with music biz buddies in 1985 with *That's What Friends Are For*. The group disbanded in 1989, although their lead singer was releasing albums as late as 2006, when she was in her seventh decade and still sounding fresh.

Founded: 1953
Origin: Atlanta, Georgia
Type: R&B, soul
Members: Langston George, Eleanor Guest, William Guest, Brenda Knight, Gladys Knight, Merald 'Bubba' Knight, Edward Patten
Highest chart positions (Gladys Knight & the Pips): 1 US, 1 US R&B (*Midnight Train To Georgia*, 1973); 1 US R&B (*Every Beat Of My Heart*, 1961, *I Heard It Through The Grapevine*, 1967, *If I Were Your Woman*, 1970, *Neither One Of Us (Wants To Be The First To Say Goodbye)* and *I've Got To Use My Imagination*, both 1973, *Best Thing That Ever Happened To Me*, 1974, *Save The Overtime (For Me)*, 1983, *Love Overboard*, 1987); 4 UK (*The Way We Were – Try To Remember*, 1975, *Baby Don't Change Your Mind*, 1977)
Highest chart positions (Gladys Knight): 1 US, 1 US R&B (*That's What Friends Are For* with Dionne Warwick, Elton John and Stevie Wonder, 1985); 6 UK (*Licence To Kill*, 1989)

Stacy Lattisaw

Stacy Lattisaw was just 13 when she made it to the peak of the US dance charts with two consecutive singles – *Dynamite!* and *Jump To The Beat* – in 1980. Her next release, *Let Me Be Your Angel*, crossed over on to the mainstream chart and it all looked very good indeed for the young Washington singer and her label, Cotillion. It had all come about through her association with producer Michael Walden, a former drummer in John McLaughlin's Mahavishnu Orchestra. She was in and out of the Billboard Hot 100 over the next few years, and it looked like a no-brainer for Motown when they had the chance to sign Lattisaw, still a teenager, in 1986. Hadn't she cross-genre appeal, and hadn't she opened for the Jacksons on their Triumph tour of 1981? Her first Motown album, *Take Me All The Way*, produced a mid-range hit in *Nail It To The Wall*, but the second, *Personal Attention*, contained only R&B chart successes. The third, *What You Need*, however, gave birth to a number one

R&B hit in collaboration with Johnny Gill, *Where Do We Go From Here*. But Lattisaw's disenchantment with the music industry was the decisive factor in her stepping back and concentrating on her family. She has now gone back to her roots and focuses on gospel music.

Left: *Stacy Lattisaw – a number one R&B hit with Johnny Gill*

Born: 25 November 1966, Washington, DC
Type: R&B, soul, pop, gospel
Highest chart positions: 21 US (*Let Me Be Your Angel*, 1980); 1 US R&B (*Where Do We Go From Here* with Johnny Gill, 1989); 3 UK (*Jump To The Beat*, 1980)

Shorty Long

Frederick Earl Long was a one-hit wonder in the UK but a three-hit thriller in the US. Earning his nickname through his diminutive stature (just over five feet in his stockinged feet), Long made the Hot 100 with *Function At The Junction* (1966), *Night Fo' Last* (1968) and the song that made his name in Britain, *Here Comes The Judge*. At one point in the summer of 1968 it seemed as if every single Briton was strutting around with elbows pumping and proclaiming: 'Here comes the judge, here comes the judge'. It was one of the funkiest records to chart in Britain up to that point, and emphasised that Long was born to funk. He was a multi-instrumentalist and a DJ who had toured with the Ink Spots when, in 1959, he moved to Detroit and cut records for Harvey Fuqua's Tri-Phi label. When Fuqua sold up to Berry Gordy, Long became a Motown man. *Devil With A Blue Dress On* (1964) was the first record issued on Motown's Soul label, and was later a hit for Detroit rocker Mitch Ryder. Despite the

excellence of his recordings, Long had to wait until 1966 for his first hit. Then came 1968, but just a year later Long was dead, drowned in a boating accident on the Detroit River. Stevie Wonder played harmonica in tribute at his funeral.

Born: 20 May 1940, Birmingham, Alabama
Died: 29 June 1969, Detroit, Michigan
Type: R&B, soul
Highest chart positions: 8 US, 4 US R&B (*Here Comes The Judge*, 1968); 30 UK (*Here Comes The Judge*)

The Marvelettes

To the Marvelettes goes the accolade of being the first artists to take Motown to the top of the Billboard Hot 100. They did it in 1961 with *Please Mr Postman*, a song in which group member Georgia Dobbins – who left the group before it was recorded – had had a hand in writing. The record, issued on the Tamla label, set a poppy standard that the group strove hard to live up to, but it was to be their only number one; this despite the best efforts of songwriting and production helpers like Smokey Robinson, Holland-Dozier-Holland, Marvin Gaye and Ashford-Simpson. The group had come into being when schoolfriends Dobbins, Gladys Horton, Katherine Anderson, Georgeanna Tillman and Juanita Cowart got together and performed at their school's glee club in 1960. Wanda Young replaced Dobbins before the group signed to Motown and over the years they went through several line-ups. The big problem facing the Marvelettes' took the form of label-mates the Supremes, who seemed just that little bit classier and were treated to a bigger promotional effort. Still, they racked up a good few hits, and as late as 1966 were penetrating the top 10 with *Don't Mess With Bill*. The group broke up in the early 70s.

Left: *The Marvelettes – took Motown to the top of the pop chart for the first time*

Founded: 1960

Origin: Inkster, Michigan

Type: R&B, soul, doo-wop, pop

Members: Katherine Anderson, Ann Bogan, Juanita Cowart, Georgia Dobbins, Gladys Horton, Wanda Rogers, Georgeanna Tillman

Highest chart positions: 1 US, 1 US R&B (*Please Mr Postman*, 1961); 13 UK (*When You're Young And In Love*, 1967)

The Mary Jane Girls

The Mary Jane Girls were a product of funkmeister Rick James's imagination – and what an imagination it proved to be. Even the band's name was an indicator of James's predilection for certain products of the cannabis plant. The Motown man dreamed up cheeky characters for each of the members after recruiting them as backing singers for his Stone City Band, and was the songwriting and production force behind the band's first album, *Mary Jane Girls* (1983). Four singles from the album knocked at the door of the Hot 100 without gaining entry, although three of them, including *All Night Long*, performed better in the UK. James resumed his duties for the next album, *Only Four You* (1985), by which time Yvette Marine had replaced Ann Bailey. Out of that record came the group's biggest American seller, *In My House*, a number one on the dance chart, and *Wild And Crazy Love*, which did almost as well. The only time James relinquished his songwriting grip on the Mary Jane Girls, they charted with a cover of Bob Crewe and Bob Gaudio's *Walk Like A Man*, previously a hit for the Four Seasons. When James and Motown fell out, the Mary Jane Girls fell apart.

Founded: 1979
Origin: Los Angeles, California
Type: R&B, soul, funk
Members: Cheryl Ann 'Cheri' Bailey, Candice 'Candi' Ghant, Joanne 'JoJo' McDuffie, Yvette 'Corvette' Marine, Kimberly 'Maxi' Wuletich
Highest chart positions: 7 US, 3 US R&B (*In My House*, 1985); 13 UK (*All Night Long*, 1983)

Michael McDonald

Few people would associate Steely Dan and the Doobie Brothers with Motown, yet that is the trail Michael McDonald followed. If the Doobies' gently rolling sing-alongs typified the Californian soft rock scene of the 1970s, when McDonald joined their ranks there was a definite move to a more jazzy, soulful sound, and in truth his blue-eyed soul was ideally suited to Motown. He had contributed backing vocals to Steely Dan albums before he joined the Doobies in 1977, and before he left he had also sung on hit singles by the likes of Donna Summer and Christopher Cross. His first solo album, *If That's What It Takes* (1982), contained a song in *I Keep Forgettin'* that took him into the US top five, his highest position ever, and another (*I Gotta Try*) that broke into the top 50. The hits continued sporadically until 2003, when he began a project with Motown that would see him covering classic songs from the label's history. McDonald's version of *Ain't No Mountain High Enough*, from the *Motown* album, was a big hit on the adult contemporary scene and the history lesson continued in 2004 with *Motown Two*. Four years later came the *Soul Speak* album, which included a minor R&B hit in *Love TKO* and a bigger one in the adult contemporary chart, *(Your Love Keeps Lifting Me) Higher And Higher*.

Below: *Michael McDonald – covered classic songs from Motown's history*

Born: 12 February 1952, St Louis, Missouri
Type: Soul, rock
Highest chart positions: 1 US, 1 US R&B (*On My Own* with Patti LaBelle, 1986); 1 UK (*On My Own*)

Brian McKnight

Once he'd changed labels from Mercury to Motown, Brian McKnight's albums just couldn't help charting, and doing it remarkably consistently. Starting in October 1998 with *Bethlehem* (aimed at the Christmas market), McKnight followed up with *Back At One* (1999, triple platinum sales), *Superhero* (2001, rated gold) and *U Turn* (2003, also gold), all three of which peaked at number seven on the Billboard 200. He went three better when he released *Gemini*, which finished up at number four and gave rise to two singles that breached the R&B top 40. After he left Motown the momentum slowed a little. McKnight is a man of many talents: apart from his remarkable falsetto vocal range, he can offer songwriting, arranging and production skills, and he's a multi-instrumentalist with piano, percussion, guitar, trombone, tuba and flugelhorn strings, as it were, to his bow. He's also the possessor of the remarkable number of 16 Grammy Award nominations although he's never made it to the winner's rostrum. Oh yes, and he has also played basketball to a high level. It all came so easily to McKnight, who grew up in a musical family and had secured a publishing deal by the time he was 18. Fame was sure to follow, and he continues to produce high quality, with the album *More Than Words* being released in 2013.

> **Born:** 5 June 1969, Buffalo, New York
> **Type:** R&B, soul
> **Highest chart positions:** 2 US (*Back At One*, 1999); 4 US R&B (*You Should Be Mine (Don't Waste Your Time)*, 1997); 36 UK (*You Should Be Mine (Don't Waste Your Time)*)

Barbara McNair

Barbara McNair will always be better known as an actress than as a singer, yet it was as a highly talented vocalist that she came to notice, and her spell at Motown will linger long in the memory. Upon moving to New York after a spell at the American Conservatory of Music and a year at university, McNair auditioned for nightclub gigs all over the city and got her break when she clinched a booking at the Village Vanguard. From there she graduated to a deal with Coral Records and appearances on *The Ed Sullivan Show* among other programmes. While she was making her recording debut with *Till There Was You* (1958), she was also making her first forays into the world of acting, appearing in *The Body Beautiful* and *The Pajama* Game on Broadway. Things were happening fast for McNair; she toured with Nat King Cole and signed for the Signature label in 1960, made ever more frequent TV appearances and in 1963 marked up her first appearance on film. It was in 1965 that she moved to Motown, scoring an immediate success and her biggest hit with her first release for the label, *You're Gonna Love My Baby*. Among the songs that followed was *Baby a Go-Go*, which lay undiscovered for decades until it was picked up by Northern Soul aficionados. From 1968 onwards, McNair concentrated on her highly productive TV and acting careers.

Left: *Barbara McNair – you're gonna love her baby*

Born: 4 March 1934, Chicago, Illinois
Died: 4 February 2007, Los Angeles, California
Type: R&B, soul, jazz, pop

The Miracles

They're one of the names most readily associated with Motown, and with good reason: the Miracles were the label's first really successful group, and after they became Smokey Robinson & the Miracles in 1965 they kept the hits coming until 1976. The Detroit group began life as the Five Chimes in 1955 but by the following year, with a change in personnel, had become the Matadors. With Claudette Rogers joining in lieu of her brother Sonny, the group attracted the attention of songwriter Berry Gordy, who produced their first single *Got A Job*, issued on End Records in 1958. Soon, with another change of name, the Miracles were recording for Berry's Motown/Tamla, and hitting number two on the pop charts with *Shop Around* (1960). The top 10 hit *You've Really Got A Hold On Me* followed in 1962, and many others came in the years afterwards. The history of the Miracles is, of course, closely linked with the Smokey Robinson story, which will be examined in depth later.

Founded: 1955
Origin: Detroit, Michigan
Type: R&B, soul, doo-wop, disco, funk
Members: Carl Cotton, Clarence 'Humble' Dawson, Dave Finley, James 'Rat' Grice, Billy Griffin, Donald Griffin, Warren 'Pete' Moore, Claudette Robinson, William 'Smokey' Robinson, Emerson 'Sonny' Rogers, Robert 'Bobby' Rogers, Mark Scott, Marvin 'Marv' Tarplin, Tee Turner, Ronald 'Ronnie' White
Highest chart positions: 1 US, 1 US R&B (*The Tears Of A Clown*, 1970); 1 US (*Love Machine*, 1976); 1 US R&B (*Shop Around*, 1960, *You've Really Got A Hold On Me*, 1962, *I Second That Emotion*, 1967); 1 UK (*The Tears Of A Clown*)

The Monitors

How different things might have been for Warren Harris, who had Otis Williams and Melvin Franklin for schoolmates. The three became members of the Distants, but Harris left that group before they merged with the Primes and became the Temptations. Meanwhile, Richard Street released a single produced by Norman Whitfield, *Answer Me*, on Thelma Records as Richard Street & the Distants before he got together with Harris and John and Sandra Fagin to form the Majestics. Their first release on Motown's VIP label, which should have been *Hello Love* in 1964, was jettisoned, as was the band name: there was already a band working as the Majestics. As the Monitors, the group released *Say You*, later covered by the Temptations, in 1966 and saw it reach number 36 on the R&B chart. Better was to come: *Greetings (This Is Uncle Sam)*, airing the subject of the American army draft for service in the Vietnam War, was an R&B hit. It was followed by further singles on VIP – *Since I Lost You Girl* (1966) and *Bring Back The Love* (1968) – and one on Motown's Soul label, *Step By Step (Hand In Hand)* in 1968. A partial reunion in 1990 resulted in the release of a new album, *Grazing In The Grass*, on Ian Levine's Motorcity label.

Founded: 1964

Origin: Detroit, Michigan

Type: R&B, soul

Members: John 'Maurice' Fagin, Sandra Fagin, Leah Harris, Warren Harris, Herschel Hunter, Darrell Littlejohn, Richard Street

Highest chart positions: 100 US, 21 US R&B (*Greetings (This Is Uncle Sam)*, 1966)

Mýa

Right: *Mýa – sad tale to tell about her fourth album*

The story of Mýa Marie Harrison's fourth studio album, *Liberation*, recorded for Universal Motown and ready for release in 2005, is a strange one. Mýa had started work on an album before she left the Interscope label, for which she had provided a regular flow of album and single hits following her debut in 1998. Work on *Liberation* progressed rapidly and it was ready for release within three months, with insiders acclaiming its production and its appearances from artists like Snoop Dogg and Lil Wayne. Sadly, the economic climate in the record industry meant the album's release date was repeatedly pushed back until 2007, when the label accidentally-on-purpose leaked it in Japan. It was subsequently released as a digital download in that country and that, disappointingly, marked the end of Mýa's Universal Motown career. Which was a crying shame, for the dancer turned singer had shown immense promise as a young hit-maker and had impressed Haqq Islam enough for him to sign her to Interscope. Her first album, *Mýa*, came to public notice in 1998, when she was just 18, and promptly went platinum. Her most vivid impression on the singles charts came when she teamed up with Christina Aguilera, Lil' Kim and Pink to rework the classic *Lady Marmalade* for the soundtrack to the film *Moulin Rouge!*

Born: 10 October 1979, Washington, DC
Type: R&B, soul, hip hop, pop
Highest chart positions: 1 US (*Lady Marmalade* with Christina Aguilera, Lil' Kim and Pink, 2001); 2 US R&B (*It's All About Me* featuring Sisqó, 1998); 1 UK (*Lady Marmalade*)

Ne-Yo

It must have been gratifying for Universal Motown bosses when Ne-Yo's first album for the label, *R.E.D.*, reached number four on the Billboard 200 and the top of the R&B/hip hop album chart in late 2012. The label had, after all, appointed the singer-songwriter as its senior vice-president for A&R prior to the album's release; it showed the Arkansas man knew what he was talking about. Joking aside, *R.E.D.* (an acronym of Realising Every Dream) indicated there was a lot more to come from Ne-Yo, who had already proved himself one of the 21st century's most successful artists. Born Shaffer Chimere Smith and brought up in Las Vegas, Ne-Yo got involved in the music industry as a writer while in his teens but waited until 2006 for his first big hit – and what a hit it was. *So Sick* smashed into top 10s all over the world and was the first of four chart-toppers in Britain. *Sexy Love* and *Because Of You* have been among the other biggies, and *R.E.D.* alone has yielded four big sellers including *Let*

Left: *Ne-Yo – involved in the music industry from his teens*

Me Love You (Until You Learn To Love Yourself), another global favourite. He's liberal with his songwriting favours, bestowing hits like *Irreplaceable* and *Take A Bow* on Beyoncé and Rihanna respectively. Watch him go.

Born: 18 October 1979, Camden, Arkansas
Type: R&B, soul, hip hop, pop, dance
Highest chart positions: 1 US (*So Sick*, 2006); 1 US R&B (*Sexy Love*, 2006, *Miss Independent*, 2008); 1 UK (*So Sick*, *Closer*, 2008, *Beautiful Monster*, 2010, *Let Me Love You (Until You Learn To Love Yourself)*, 2012)

The Originals

It was appropriate that the Marvelettes' hit of 1961 should be titled *Please Mr Postman*, for Freddie Gorman, one of the writing team that gave Motown its first number one, was well schooled in the art of delivering mail. The postal worker went on to keep the label well supplied with songs and came up with a few hits for his own group, the Originals. They have often been referred to as Motown's best-kept secret, which is a fair judgment, but they did make the charts often enough to be stars in their own right. Gorman had formed the Fideletones with Brian Holland as far back as 1957, and happened to run across Berry Gordy on his mail-carrying route. The writing team of Lamont-Dozier-Gorman was productive but, when Holland's brother Eddie superseded Gorman, the latter returned to his postal duties. He resurfaced with the Originals, who benefited from the help of Marvin Gaye, the Motown icon co-writing and producing their biggest hits, *Baby I'm For Real* and *The Bells*. In the second half of the 1970s the group found a degree of success on the disco scene, but it was not to last too much longer. They broke up in 1982.

Founded: 1966

Origin: Detroit, Michigan

Type: R&B, soul, disco

Members: Hank Dixon, Terrie Dixon, Defrantz Forrest, Walter Gaines, Dillon Gorman, Freddie Gorman, Ty Hunter, CP Spencer, Joe Stubbs

Highest chart positions: 12 US (*The Bells*, 1970); 1 US R&B (*Baby, I'm For Real*, 1969)

Bonnie Pointer

She was told as a child that rock 'n' roll and the blues were the Devil's music, but Patricia Eva 'Bonnie' Pointer doesn't seem to have listened. Neither did her sisters Anita, Issa, June, Ruth and Sadako, who at various times have formed the Pointer Sisters, tasting success mostly in the 70s and 80s. It was Bonnie and youngest sister June who had begun the group as teenagers in 1969, and when sibling Ruth joined, Atlantic were convinced enough to sign the trio and start recording some music. Hits came their way, but before the Pointers' *Fire* hit the number two spot in America in 1979, youngest-but-one sister Bonnie had embarked on a solo career with Motown, having married producer Jeffrey Bowen in 1978. The following year, Bonnie's cover of the Elgins' *Heaven Must Have Sent You*, taken from the album *Bonnie Pointer (Red Album)*, peaked at number 11 on the Billboard Hot 100. The second full-length release, *Bonnie Pointer (Purple Album)*, included another cover of a well-known song in

I Can't Help Myself (Sugar Pie, Honey Bunch) – which touched number 40 – and other Motown standards. Bonnie, despite some well-publicised problems with drugs, has reunited with various sisters at different times over the years, and in 2009 started performing with Ruth and Anita plus niece Sadako.

Born: 11 July 1950, Oakland, California
Type: R&B, soul, disco
Highest chart positions: 11 US (*Heaven Must Have Sent You*, 1979); 10 US R&B (*Free Me From My Freedom / Tie Me To A Tree (Handcuff Me)*, 1979)

Billy Preston

Billy Preston was a child prodigy, playing keyboards with the gospel phenomenon Mahalia Jackson at the age of 10 and featuring in the Hollywood biopic *WC Handy* two years later. He became a musician's musician, playing and recording with everyone from Ray Charles, Little Richard and Sam Cooke to the Beatles and the Red Hot Chili Peppers and, meanwhile, developing his own recording career very nicely, thank you. He was in fact still at high school when his debut album, *16 Yr Old Soul*, came out in 1963. His Beatles connection meant Preston's solo releases in 1969 and 1970 were on the band's Apple Label, but he switched to A&M in 1971 and then, in 1979, to Motown. He'd already notched up two number one singles, but at Motown he teamed with Syreeta Wright to claim the number four spot in the US and number two in Britain with *With You I'm Born Again*. The song was taken from the album *Late At Night*, and when Preston's next album came it was a package of duets with Syreeta. The duo again proved popular with record buyers. Preston made two more albums for Motown but suffered years of personal and health problems before dying of kidney failure.

Born: 2 September 1946, Houston, Texas
Died: 6 June 2006, Scottsdale, Arizona
Type: R&B, soul, rock, disco, funk, gospel
Highest chart positions: 1 US (*Will It Go Round In Circles*, 1973, *Nothing From Nothing*, 1974); 1 US R&B (*Outa-Space*, 1972, *Space Race*, 1973); 2 UK (*With You I'm Born Again* with Syreeta Wright, 1979)

Q-Tip

Variously known as Jonathan David (his birth name), Kamaal Ibn John Fareed, Abstract and MC Love Child, the rapper Q-Tip has garnered accolades for his work with the hip hop trio A Tribe Called Quest. He formed the group with fellow students from Murray Bergtraum High School for Business Careers Ali Shaheed Muhammad and Malik Taylor (known as Phife Dawg) in 1988, and soon found himself guesting on De La Soul's album *3 Feet High and Rising*. Tribe had produced outstanding recorded work for nine years (including the best-selling album *Beats, Rhymes And Life*) when Q-Tip made his solo debut, *Amplified*, in 1999. It generated two hit singles, *Vivrant Thing* and *Breathe And Stop*, and then he got on with the business of working with myriad other artists and recording on his own, without ever being able to release the results. That changed in 2008, when *The Renaissance* was released on Universal Motown. Featuring contributions from D'Angelo, Norah Jones and Raphael Saadiq, it was mostly produced by Q-Tip with help from J Dilla and the sought-after Mark Ronson, and, to an enthusiastic welcome from the critics, reached number 11 on the album charts. He continues his prolific output in collaboration with other musicians and a new solo album, *The Last Zulu*, is expected in 2014.

Above: *Q-Tip – gathered acclaim for his work with A Tribe Called Quest*

Born: 10 April 1970, Queens, New York
Type: Hip hop
Highest chart positions: 4 US (*Groove Is In The Heart* as Deee-Lite featuring Q-Tip, 1990); 3 US R&B (*Got 'Til It's Gone* as Janet Jackson featuring Q-Tip and Joni Mitchell, 1997); 2 UK (*Groove Is In The Heart*)

Queen Latifah

Below: *Queen Latifah – all hail the queen*

Dana Owens, aka Queen Latifah, led the way for female rappers in showing that the men could not have it all their own way. She was the first real female star in the genre and the first to have an album achieve gold status. Where she went other women found themselves freer to follow. She has also become a multimedia personality, appearing in films and sitcoms and even starring in her own TV talk show. Latifah (she was given the name, which means delicate, by a cousin) began rapping in high school and later, at college, worked with Afrika Bambaataa's Native Tongues collective. Signing to the Tommy Boy label in 1988, she released two well-received albums – *All Hail The Queen* and *Nature Of A Sista* – and got involved with the collective and management company Flavor Unit. Then, in 1993, she released the album *Black Reign* on Motown, and it obliged by climbing to number 60 on the Billboard 200 and supplying her first three hits on the mainstream US chart (she had already had singles success in the UK). One of the hits was *U.N.I.T.Y.*, which addressed the issue of disrespect to women (listen up, male hip hoppers) and won a Grammy Award for Best Rap Solo Performance. The Motown album *She's The Queen*, released in 2002, showcases all Latifah's hits up to that point.

Born: 18 March 1970, Newark, New Jersey
Type: Hip hop, soul, jazz, gospel
Highest chart positions: 23 US, 7 US R&B (*U.N.I.T.Y.*, 1994); 14 UK (*Mama Gave Birth To The Soul Children*, 1990)

Barbara Randolph

Barbara Randolph followed her mother, blues singer and actress Lillian Randolph, into show business at the age of eight, appearing in the 1953 Harry Belafonte film *Bright Road*. Four years later, mother and daughter joined relation Steve Gibson's group the Red Caps as singers, and by 1960 Barbara was recording as a solo singer for RCA. In 1964 her talent was sufficiently recognised for her to replace Zola Taylor in the Platters (leaving after recording one album), and she was continuing to work as an actress. The year of 1967 was a good one, for it was then that Randolph played the part of Dorothy in hit movie *Guess Who's Coming To Dinner* alongside acting giants Spencer Tracy, Katharine Hepburn and Sidney Poitier, and signed a deal with Motown. Two singles appeared on the Soul label – *I Got A Feeling* and *Can I Get A Witness* – and there was talk in 1967 of Randolph replacing Florence Ballard in the Supremes, but Randolph was destined not to become a successful recording

Left: *Barbara Randolph – her records are favourites on the Northern Soul scene*

artist. On stage, though, it was a different matter. She toured with Marvin Gaye as a stand-in for an ill Tammi Terrell as well as with the Four Tops, Gladys Knight & the Pips and Hugh Masekela in the Motown Sound show of 1968. Thereafter she concentrated on her production company, run with husband Eddie Singleton (former spouse of Berry Gordy's ex Raynoma Liles). Randolph's records are favourites of Northern Soul fans.

Born: 5 May 1942, Detroit, Michigan
Died: 15 July 2002, South Africa
Type: R&B, soul

Rare Earth

Below: *Rare Earth – had a label named after them*

The Rochester, New York band Rustix may or may not have been the first all-white combo to be signed by Motown; it may have been Rare Earth. What is certain is that the latter outfit were Motown's first white band to achieve success – they even managed to get the company to name its rock label after them. Rare Earth (the band) had their origins in the Detroit R&B band the Sunliners, who did the rounds of the club circuit for year after weary year without getting a deal. Once they had changed their name and signed for Verve they issued the album *Dreams/Answers* (1968), which was not a success. Their first on the Rare Earth label, *Get Ready* (1970), however, zoomed up the R&B chart to number four and settled at 12 on the Billboard 200. The single from which the album took its name did even better, reaching number four on the Hot 100. The next album, *Ecology* (1970), included two hit singles in *(I Know) I'm Losing You* and *Born To Wander*, but the band's day in the sun was too brief. They finally broke up in 1978, although a version of the group still tours.

Founded: 1960
Origin: Detroit, Michigan
Type: Rock, soul
Members: Gil Bridges, Mike Bruner, Randy 'Bird' Burghdoff, Dan Ferguson, Eddie Guzman, Peter Hoorelbeke, Kenny James, Jerry Lacroix, Reggie McBride, Ray Monette, Mark Olson, John Persh, Rod Richards, Pete Rivera, Floyd Stokes Jr, Mike Urso, Paul Warren
Highest chart positions: 4 US, 20 US R&B (*Get Ready*, 1970); 20 US R&B (*(I Know) I'm Losing You*, 1970)

Martha Reeves & The Vandellas

If there was ever a girl group within the Motown house that was capable of challenging the might of Diana Ross and the Supremes, it was Martha & the Vandellas. Featuring the glorious, blues-gospel vocals of Martha Reeves, the group swung, swayed and sang their way to a succession of big sellers that had every guy grabbing a girl, everywhere around the world. Everyone was, it appeared, ready for a brand new beat. It all started to come together in Detroit when Rosalind Ashford and Annette Beard, together with lead vocalist Gloria Williams, were singing in a group named the Del-Phis. When one member left the six-strong group, a young lady called Martha Reeves, previously with rival outfits the Fascinations and the Sabre-Ettes, took her place. The Del-Phis seemed to be going places and recorded

for Checker Records and Checkmate, but the records did nothing. Reeves, hoping to win a contract with Motown, left to go solo under the name of Martha LaVaille but showed up on the wrong day for an audition arranged with the label's Mickey Stevenson. Instead of a recording contract, she landed the job of Stevenson's secretary. By now the group, under the name of the Vels, were doing backing vocals for Motown acts like

Below: *Martha Reeves – from Mickey Stevenson's secretary to singing superstar*

MARTHA REEVES & THE VANDELLAS

Above: *Martha Reeves & the Vandellas – they were dancing in the street despite the heatwave*

Marvin Gaye. When Mary Wells failed to show for a recording session, in stepped the Vels with Reeves on lead vocals, and boss Berry Gordy was so impressed he offered the group a contract. The prospect of the showbiz grind was not appealing to Williams, who opted out, leaving a trio who renamed themselves the Vandellas. As luck would have it, the Holland-Dozier-Holland team was limbering up just as the contract was signed, and their first composition and production, *Come And Get These Memories*, became a hit for Martha & the Vandellas on the Gordy label in 1963. The next record, *(Love Is Like A) Heat Wave*, struck the US like a tornado, hurtling to number four on the Hot 100 and earning a Grammy nomination. Thereafter, hit followed hit with *Quicksand*, *Live Wire* and *In My Lonely Room* keeping the pot boiling until the group's success

hit new heights with the 1964 song for which they are best known: *Dancing In The Street*. When it was reissued in the UK in 1969, the Marvin Gaye, Mickey Stevenson, Ivy Jo Hunter song provided the Vandellas' first transatlantic hit. The group – who had one or two personnel changes and became Martha *Reeves &* the Vandellas in 1967, confirming the lead singer's prominence – hardly ever failed to make the Hot 100 until 1973, when *Baby Don't Leave Me* flopped. Before that failure, infighting among the group and Motown's promotional focus on other acts had taken the sheen off their popularity. In 1974, Reeves left Motown for MCA and the dancing in the street came to an end.

Founded: 1962
Origin: Detroit, Michigan
Type: R&B, soul, doo-wop, rock 'n' roll, pop
Members: Rosalind Ashford-Holmes, Annette Beard-Helton, Betty Kelly, Lois Reeves, Martha Reeves, Sandra Tilley, Gloria Williams
Highest chart positions: 2 US (*Dancing In The Street*, 1964); 1 US R&B (*(Love Is Like A) Heat Wave*, 1963, *Jimmy Mack*, 1967); 4 UK (*Dancing In The Street*)

Lionel Richie

As documented earlier, Lionel Richie struck out on his own, leaving the Commodores after he had scored a worldwide hit in *Endless Love* with Diana Ross. It was the beginning of a remarkable solo career that saw him dominate the charts for the best part of a decade in a way that few artists have ever emulated. Richie had joined the Commodores at college in Tuskegee, Oklahoma and, as vocalist, saxophonist and songwriter he had shared the fruits of the group's Motown triumphs. It was in 1981 that, with tensions mounting in the band due to his solo success, he set sail on his own, and his first Motown album, *Lionel Richie* (1982), confirmed the correctness of his decision. Selling more than four million, it contained three top five hits including *Truly*, his first number one. The next album, *Can't Slow Down* (1983), fared even better, selling an extraordinary 10 million copies and giving birth to five top 10 singles including *Hello*, which became his first UK chart-topper. Richie went on recording for Motown until 1986, when *Dancing On The Ceiling* continued the platinum sales story. Then he quit while he was winning, not returning to the studio until 1996 for the Mercury label. It had been great while it lasted.

Left: *Lionel Richie – unlike the Vandellas, he was dancing on the ceiling*

> **Born:** 20 June 1949, Tuskegee, Alabama
> **Type:** R&B, soul, pop, rock
> **Highest chart positions:** 1 US, 1 US R&B (*Endless Love* with Diana Ross, 1981, *All Night Long (All Night)*, 1983, *Hello*, 1984, *Say You, Say Me*, 1985); 1 US (*Truly*, 1982); 1 US R&B (*Do It To Me*, 1992); 1 UK (*Hello*)

Smokey Robinson

If anyone believes the story of William 'Smokey' Robinson is mostly the story of Smokey Robinson & the Miracles, they are way off the mark. The truth of the matter is that without Smokey, Motown would not have been half the powerhouse it turned out to be. Sure, he was one of the first artists to sign up to Berry Gordy's dream as part of the Miracles and, sure, he contributed many a hit record to the label's catalogue as leader of that band and as a solo artist, but he also did much more. Robinson was a behind-the scenes miracle-performer, working in his capacity as vice-president to find new artists, train them in the Motown method and groom them for stardom, and writing and producing the hits many of the acts were grateful to be given. And when he left the Miracles he continued to record,

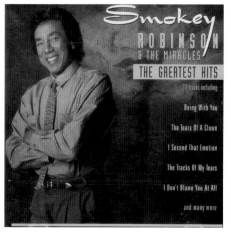

chalking up hits until as late as 1991. The man whom Bob Dylan was later to call America's greatest living poet grew up listening to jazz and blues and started his music career singing doo-wop. The group that was to become the Miracles, the Five Chimes, came together in 1955, and three years later Robinson met a young songwriter who was intent on making a big impression on the business. He urged Berry Gordy (for it was he) to form the label he kept talking about, and when Motown came into being the Miracles were the first artists to sign. *Shop Around* (1960) became the nascent label's first national hit and it was followed by a string of others: *Going To A Go-Go, Oo Baby Baby, The Tracks Of My Tears, I Second That Emotion, The Tears Of A Clown* … the list goes on and on. Meanwhile, Robinson was taking his duties as Motown v-p seriously, writing winners like *My Guy* (Mary Wells), *My Girl* and *Get Ready* (the Temptations) and *Ain't That Peculiar* (Marvin Gaye), doing more than his

Left & Far Left:
Smokey Robinson – a behind-the-scenes miracle worker as well as a star performer

fair share of production shifts and all the while scouring the scene for fresh talent to bring to Gordy's notice. When it came to the end of his road with the Miracles he took a year off, then returned to the studio to record the album *Smokey* (1973). As a solo artist he took a long time to take a single to the US top 10; it happened in 1979 with *Cruisin'*, then it happened again with *Being With You* and *Just To See Her* (1987). That year was when he was inducted into the Rock & Roll Hall of Fame (and no one deserved it more) but changes were looming. In 1988 Motown was sold to MCA and Robinson deemed it the right time for a parting of the ways, but not before he had recorded one more album: *Love, Smokey*. Following a troubled period in his life, he returned to his first love when MCA revived Motown, releasing the *Intimate* album (1999). Smokey remains one of America's best-loved heroes.

Born: 19 February 1940, Detroit, Michigan
Type: R&B, soul, pop
Highest chart positions as a solo artist: 2 US (*Being With You*, 1981); 1 US R&B (*Baby That's Backatcha*, 1975, *Being With You*, 1981); 1 UK (*Being With You*)

Rockwell

Right:
*Somebody's
Watching Me by
Rockwell – famous
names helped out
in the recording*

He was named Kennedy William Gordy after President John F Kennedy and William 'Smokey' Robinson, but the boy who became Rockwell was never one to trade on his connections. The son of Berry Gordy and Margaret Norton managed to get a record deal with Motown behind his famous father's back, and changed his name in order to divert accusations of nepotism. In addition, he believed in his ability to rock well, and record buyers agreed with that judgment. But he couldn't resist getting star names into the studio to help out when it came to recording his first album, *Somebody's Watching Me*: Michael and Jermaine Jackson supplied backing vocals for the single of the same name, which related Rockwell's fear of being followed and almost made it to the top of the Billboard Hot 100. The follow-up single, *Obscene Phone Caller*, broke into the top 40 and the UK's top 100 but the next two, *Knife* and George Harrison's *Taxman*, did nothing much. However, the album had made the former Kennedy Gordy the family's most successful recording artist by some distance. Next up was another album, *Captured* (1985), from which *He's A Cobra* was a minor R&B hit, and then came *The Genie* (1986). It turned out that Rockwell was pretty much a one-album kind of guy, but at least he did it under his own name.

Born: 15 March 1964, Detroit, Michigan
Type: R&B, pop
Highest chart positions: 2 US, 1 US R&B (*Somebody's Watching Me*, 1983); 6 UK (*Somebody's Watching Me*)

Diana Ross

Most people would be content with one Motown career. Diana Ross, history's most successful female entertainer according to the *Guinness Book Of World Records*, has had three: one with the Supremes, the group that perhaps did most to communicate the sound of young America to the world; another as a mega-selling solo artist between 1970 and 1981; and yet another, between 1988 and 2001, back with the label that had originally brought her fame. In all that time, Ross showed unique qualities of stage presence, showwomanship and spine-tingling vocal skills. Oh yes, and she's an acclaimed actress, too. She began her rise to superstardom as part of the Primettes, a four-piece vocal group, in 1959 when she was just 15. That group became the Supremes and helped to change the face of music. Having scored yet another huge hit with *Someday We'll Be Together* in 1969, Ross took the momentous step of going solo and she was teamed up with one of Motown's top writing/

production partnerships, Nickolas Ashford and Valerie Simpson. It didn't take long for the Ross-Ashford-Simpson team to start producing the goods: *Reach Out And Touch (Somebody's Hand)* (1970) rose to number 20 on the Hot 100 and 33 in the UK. Next came a massive worldwide seller, *Ain't No Mountain High Enough*, and another top 20 song in the shape of *Remember Me*. In 1971, Ross notched up her first UK number one, *I'm Still Waiting*, written by Deke Richards. By 1972 she was being nominated for an Oscar for her performance as jazz queen

Below: *Diana Ross – stage presence, showwomanship and spine-tingling vocal skills took her to the top*

Billie Holiday in *Lady Sings The Blues*, and a creditable cover of Holiday's *Good Morning Heartache*, taken from the film's soundtrack, was a hit. Ross's *Touch Me In The Morning* album (1973) yielded more hit singles, and three more came from *Diana & Marvin* (1973), an album of duets with Marvin Gaye. Two more movie roles came her way – in *Mahogany* (1975) and *The Wiz* (1978) – and all the while she was topping the best-sellers with regularity. Her final number one before leaving Motown for RCA was the enormous worldwide hit *Endless Love*, recorded with Lionel Richie. That proved to be Ross's final US chart-topper, but that's not to say the hits dried up; they were just of a lower magnitude. By the time she returned to Motown in 1989, however, the days of automatic top 10 placements were a thing of the past. She was still achieving big sales in Britain, but America seemed less inclined to buy Diana Ross records. No matter; Ross's status as the female entertainer of the century, awarded by *Billboard* as far back as 1976, was secure.

Born: 26 March 1944, Detroit, Michigan
Type: R&B, soul, pop, disco, jazz
Highest chart positions as a solo artist: 1 US, 1 US R&B (*Ain't No Mountain High Enough*, 1970, *Love Hangover*, 1976, *Upside Down*, 1980, *Endless Love* with Lionel Richie, 1981); 1 US (*Touch Me In The Morning*, 1973, *Theme From Mahogany (Do You Know Where You're Going To)*, 1975); 1 US R&B (*Missing You*, 1984); 1 UK (*I'm Still Waiting*, 1971, *Chain Reaction*, 1985)

David Ruffin

Ask Rod Stewart, or Daryl Hall, or John Oates. You could ask Michael Jackson or Marvin Gaye if they were still alive. They have all rated David Ruffin as one of the greatest singers there's ever been, maybe even the greatest. Ruffin's gruff, angst-ridden vocals graced many of the Temptations' best records and took him to great heights as a solo artist. David Eli Ruffin came to worldwide notice as the lead singer on *My Girl* (1965) and enjoyed the Temps' glory days as much as anyone. But there were tensions within the group, exacerbated by Ruffin's burgeoning ego (he demanded that the group be renamed David Ruffin & the Temptations, for instance) and it was no surprise to observers when he was fired in 1968. His first solo single, *My Whole World Ended (The Moment You Left Me)*, had been intended for the group, but it took Ruffin into the US top 10. From then on he was a regular in the charts' upper reaches and made a deep impression on the disco scene of the 1970s. But his later years were troubled,

marked by spells in prison and heavy drug use. He died in 1991 following an adverse reaction to cocaine.

Above: *David Ruffin – one of the greatest singers of all time, say many stars*

Born: 18 January 1941, Whynot, Mississippi
Died: 1 June 1991, Philadelphia, Pennsylvania
Type: R&B, soul, pop, disco, gospel
Highest chart positions as a solo artist: 9 US, 1 US R&B (*Walk Away From Love*, 1976); 9 US, 2 US R&B (*My Whole World Ended (The Moment You Left Me)*, 1969); 10 UK (*Walk Away From Love*)

Jimmy Ruffin

Below: *Jimmy Ruffin – he was going to give her all the love he'd got*

David's older brother was another Ruffin who had a distinguished Motown career and frequented the charts as a solo singer. As kids, the brothers sang together in the gospel group the Dixie Nightingales and Jimmy was on hand in 1961 when Motown needed session singers. He also released singles on the subsidiary Miracle label including *Don't Feel Sorry For Me* (1961) and, after a spell in the US Army, was offered a place in the Temptations, replacing Elbridge Bryant. The job went

to brother David, however, and Jimmy went back to his solo career. His liking for a song written for the Spinners was the making of him. *What Becomes Of The Brokenhearted* (1966), written by William Weatherspoon, Paul Riser and James Dean, was a major US and UK hit (it went even higher in Britain on its re-release in 1974) and was the first of a series of triumphs. *I've Passed This Way Before* (1966), *Gonna Give Her All The Love I've Got* and *Don't You Miss Me A Little Bit Baby* (both 1967) charted, but success came more easily in the UK than in America. In the 1970s Ruffin left Motown for Polydor, and even moved to Britain to capitalise on his popularity. In contrast to David, he worked hard to counter the abuse of drugs.

> **Born:** 7 May 1939, Collinsville, Mississippi
> **Type:** R&B, soul, pop, disco
> **Highest chart positions:** 7 US, 6 US R&B (*What Becomes Of The Brokenhearted*, 1966); 4 UK (*What Becomes Of The Brokenhearted*, 1974)

The Satintones

They didn't last too long and they didn't have any hits, but the Satintones can claim to be the first group to record for Motown. Sonny Sanders and Robert Bateman were employed as backing vocalists when Berry Gordy established Tamla Records in 1959. The duo tried to recruit Brian Holland to form a group but the soon-to-be-famous songwriter couldn't find the time to attend rehearsals, so attention switched to another writer, Chico Leverett, and the new group signed for Motown. They beat the Miracles to the title of first Motown group by recording *Going To The Hop* and releasing it on Tamla in July 1959. Some say the name of the record's B-side, *Motor City*, influenced Gordy's choice of title for his Motown operation a few months later. Another single, *My Beloved*, followed in October and that was it until 1961, when the planned release of *Tomorrow And Always* was abandoned because of legal moves: the song was alleged to owe much to the Shirelles' *Will You Still Love Me Tomorrow?* Instead,

Angel saw the light of day in May, to be followed by *I Know How It Feels* (June) and the Broadway song *Zing! Went The Strings Of My Heart* (October). By this time, Leverett had left and been replaced by Vernon Williams and Sammy Mack. The group disbanded in 1961, although they reunited for sessions with Ian Levine for his Motorcity project in the 1980s.

Founded: 1959
Origin: Detroit, Michigan
Type: R&B, soul, doo-wop
Members: Robert Bateman, Jimmy Ellis, Charles 'Chico' Leverett, Sammy Mack, Sonny Sanders, Vernon Williams

Shanice

SHANICE

Right: *Shanice – reaches the very highest notes a human can produce*

Shanice Lorraine Wilson-Knox has a quite extraordinary vocal talent that enables her to climb into what's known as the whistle register – the highest notes a human can produce. But that's not the only remarkable thing about this Grammy-nominated singer-songwriter who was a regular fixture in the Billboard charts from the 80s to the late 90s. When she was very young, Shanice moved to Los Angeles with her mother and aunt, who were at first intent on making it in the music business themselves but soon decided to focus on the abilities of their young charge. Just eight years old, she appeared with Ella Fitzgerald in a TV commercial and found other small screen work, and she was only 14 when A&M released her first album, *Discovery*, in 1987. While it contained three R&B hits, it didn't perform as well as Shanice's debut album for Motown, *Inner Child* (1991). That record produced her best-known song, the infectious *I Love Your Smile*, which claimed the number two spot on both the Hot 100 and the UK chart. Indeed, it broke into the top 10 in no

fewer than 22 countries. Also on the album was a version of the Minnie Riperton hit *Lovin' You*, showcasing the singer's mastery of the whistle register. Shanice's only other foray into the US top 10 came in 1993, when she recorded *It's For You* for the soundtrack of *The Meteor Man*.

Born: 14 May 1973, Pittsburgh, Pennsylvania
Type: R&B, soul, urban
Highest chart positions: 2 US, 1 US R&B (*I Love Your Smile*, 1991); 2 UK (*I Love Your Smile*)

Sharissa

Dubbed Little Stevie Wonder by her father, Sharissa Dawes was a precocious youngster. From the age of seven she wanted to do nothing other than sing, and she proceeded to do so for the benefit of her neighbours in Brooklyn and the Bronx and fellow students at junior high and high school. Her inspiration came from singers like Whitney Houston, Stephanie Mills, Patti LaBelle, Gladys Knight and Deniece Williams, and she rounded out her musical education by listening to hip hop greats Grandmaster Flash and the Sugarhill Gang. Also on the agenda were TV specials featuring some of the top Motown artists, whom Sharissa would aim to emulate. She was still only knee high to a Grandmaster when she joined a group, Triple Dose, and then another, 4Kast, in 1995. With this outfit she released the album *Any Weather* (1998). When the group sundered Sharissa was snapped up by Motown and got to work on what would become her debut album, *No Half Steppin'*, released in 2002. While the title track made some

Left: *Sharissa – all she wanted to do was sing*

noise on the R&B chart, it was *Any Other Night* that really got her noticed, reaching number 72 on the Hot 100. As happens so often, a move away from Motown proved to be to the detriment of her career, and her next work for Virgin, *Every Beat Of My Heart*, has never been released in the USA.

Born: 1976, Brooklyn, New York
Type: R&B, urban
Highest chart positions: 72 US, 23 US R&B (*Any Other Night*, 2001)

The Spinners

Below: *The Spinners – what could have been if they had stayed at Motown?*

The history of one of soul's greatest groups goes back to the mid-1950s, when friends Billy Henderson, Henry Fambrough, Pervis Jackson, CP Spencer and Bobby Smith sang together as the Domingoes. With George Dixon replacing Spencer, the group renamed themselves the Spinners (no connection to the British folk ensemble) and had hits in 1961 with *That's What Girls Are For* and *Love (I'm So Glad) I Found You* on Harvey Fuqua's Tri-Phi label. When Berry Gordy acquired Tri-Phi the Spinners became Motown artists, but hits proved hard to come by with the exception of *I'll Always Love You* (1965). It's no credit to Motown that the group were employed as road managers and chauffeurs while other outfits received much closer attention. In 1970, after the Stevie Wonder song *It's A Shame* had charted, the Spinners left Motown, signed with Atlantic and went on to achieve massive chart recognition. For Motown, they were the ones that got away.

Also known as: the Detroit Spinners, the Motown Spinners
Founded: 1954
Origin: Detroit, Michigan
Type: R&B, soul, pop, doo-wop
Members: Harold 'Spike' Bonhart, GC Cameron, George W Dixon, Chico Edwards, Jonathan Edwards, Henry Fambrough, Billy Henderson, Pervis Jackson, Bobbie Smith, CP Spencer, Joe Stubbs, Frank Washington, Philippe Wynne
Highest chart positions: 1 US, 2 US R&B (*Then Came You* with Dionne Warwick, 1974); 1 US R&B (*I'll Be Around, Could It Be I'm Falling In Love*, both 1972, *One Of A Kind (Love Affair)*, 1973, *Mighty Love (Part 1)*, 1974, *Games People Play*, 1975, *The Rubberband Man*, 1976); 1 UK (*Working My Way Back To You*, 1979)

Edwin Starr

The man who became known for his angry, scornful protest song *War* was born Charles Edwin Hatcher and as a youngster formed a doo-wop group called the Futuretones. Once he'd got his military service out of the way, Starr struggled to restart his music career but, signing for Motown's Detroit competitor Ric-Tic, released his composition *Agent Double-O-Soul* in 1965. It was a hit, and it was followed a year later by another *Stop Her On Sight (SOS)*, so Berry Gordy was delighted to have got his hands on an established star when he bought Ric-Tic in 1968. Starr pleased him even more when *25 Miles* broke into the US top 10, but it was when the singer began working with Norman Whitfield that things took off to a different level. Whitfield's *War* found precisely the right interpretation in Starr's throaty, insistent delivery and the song became a classic. Another hit came his way when *Funky Music Sho' Nuff Turns Me On* (1971) went high on the R&B chart but, sadly, his Motown days were numbered: the

Above: *Edwin Starr – what was war good for? Absolutely nothing*

company had other promotional fish to fry and his last recording for the label was *Who's Right Or Wrong*. Other hits came along, but eventually Starr moved to Britain, where he had a big following. Sadly, it was also where he suffered a heart attack and died.

Born: 21 January 1942, Nashville, Tennessee
Died: 2 April 2003, Bramcote, Nottinghamshire
Type: R&B, soul, disco, funk
Highest chart positions: 1 US, 3 US R&B (*War*, 1970); 3 UK (*War*)

Barrett Strong

In a book that contains many firsts, here's another: Barrett Strong. He was the first artist to have a hit record for Berry Gordy's young Motown operation when he broke into the Billboard Hot 100 with *Money (That's What I Want)* in 1960. Strong also turned out to be an excellent songwriter, joining forces with Norman Whitfield to produce some of Motown's best compositions. But years before that, he had become one of the first artists to sign up with Motown, and was happy when Gordy and Janie

Bradford's ditty about the love of cash was released on the Tamla label. To the delight of the young Motown team, the record received some airplay, and when it was leased to the Anna label it became a hit. The strength of the song was confirmed when it was covered in later years by, among many other artists, the Beatles and Buddy Guy. It was in the middle of the decade that the Strong-Whitfield songwriting double act came into being, with the Temptations among the groups to benefit. They wrote such Motown classics as *I Heard It Through The Grapevine*, Edwin Starr's *War* and Temptations hits like *Ball Of Confusion (That's What The World Is Today)* and *Papa Was A Rollin' Stone*, the last of which won Strong a Grammy.

Born: 5 February 1941, West Point, Mississippi
Type: R&B, soul
Highest chart positions: 23 US, 2 US R&B (*Money (That's What I Want)*, 1960)

The Supremes

Not many acts came close to rivalling the Beatles for popularity and record sales in the 1960s. In fact, only one did: the Supremes. The Detroit trio could not be matched in the sphere of girl vocal groups, and they still can't. They were Motown's numero uno act; they boasted 12 Billboard chart-toppers; they had five number ones in a row in a 1964/65 purple patch; they were America's most successful performers of the 1960s; and they are still the country's top-selling vocal group. They were the best ever example of the crossover between R&B, soul and pop music. All in all, not bad for a group of girls who met in Detroit's Brewster-Douglass housing projects in the late 1950s. At first they were a quartet, with Barbara Martin in addition to the three who would become famous: Florence Ballard, Diana Ross and Mary Wilson. Known as the Primettes (intended to be a female version of the Primes), they recorded a single, *Tears Of Sorrow*, for the Lu Pine label in 1960. It was a label that had been created especially for the group as their desire to record for Motown had been denied by Berry Gordy, who felt they were too young. The Primettes took to hanging round the Motown studios until Gordy relented enough to allow them to contribute backing vocals to some sessions. Eventually he buckled and signed them up, on condition that they change their name. Martin left the group to start a family and the Supremes were born. The first two singles went nowhere; the next six

Below: *The Supremes – still, after all this time, the USA's top-selling vocal group*

Above: *The Supremes – no fewer than 12 Billboard number ones*

floated around the lower depths of the charts; and then, in 1964, the group released the Holland-Dozier-Holland song *Where Did Our Love Go* and it all went crazy for the next few years. By 1964, Ross had taken on all the lead vocal duties and was patently the star. She it was who received the lion's share of attention, at the expense of others in the group and at the label. In 1967 Ballard was replaced by Cindy Birdsong (and after years of poverty ended up dying in 1976) and the group became Diana Ross & the Supremes. Within three years Ross had departed for her inevitable solo career and the group recruited Jean Terrell to replace her, continuing as an act – and a very good one – until 1977. But those heady days of the 1960s could never be recaptured.

Founded: 1959
Origin: Detroit, Michigan
Type: R&B, soul, doo-wop, pop, disco
Members: Florence Ballard, Cindy Birdsong, Susaye Greene, Lynda Laurence, Betty McGlown, Barbara Martin, Scherrie Payne, Diana Ross, Jean Terrell, Mary Wilson

Highest chart positions: 1 US, 1 US R&B (*Back In My Arms Again*, 1965, *You Can't Hurry Love* and *You Keep Me Hangin' On*, both 1966, *Love Is Here And Now You're Gone*, 1967, *Someday We'll Be Together*, 1969); 1 US (*Where Did Our Love Go, Baby Love* and *Come See About Me*, all 1964, *Stop! In The Name Of Love* and *I Hear A Symphony*, both 1965, *The Happening*, 1967, *Love Child*, 1968); 1 US R&B (*Stoned Love*, 1970); 1 UK (*Baby Love*)

Syreeta

It's funny how people who started working at Motown as secretaries sometimes ended up as stars. Where Martha Reeves led, Syreeta Wright followed, although Reeves never got to know Stevie Wonder quite as well as Syreeta did. The aspiring young singer had a stroke of luck when her parents moved to Detroit, and she made the most of it. Her secretarial work turned into sessions as a backing vocalist on Holland-Dozier–Holland productions and then, in 1968, a shot at stardom with the song *I Can't Give Back The Love I Feel For You*. No further records followed until 1972, but in the meantime Syreeta had met and married Wonder, who took her into new realms as a lyricist when he started setting her poems to music. The songwriting collaboration outlived the marriage, and among their hits was Wonder's *Signed, Sealed, Delivered I'm Yours* (1970). The team also came up with Syreeta winners like *Your Kiss Is Sweet* (1975), a bigger favourite in the Britain than in the US, as was often

the case. Later, she duetted with Billy Preston on the 1979 ballad *With You I'm Born Again*, but retired from music in the mid-80s. She fell victim to breast cancer in 2004.

Above: *Syreeta – with Billy Preston she was born again*

> **Born:** 3 August 1946, Pittsburgh, Pennsylvania
> **Died:** 6 July 2004, Los Angeles, California
> **Type:** R&B, soul
> **Highest chart positions:** 4 US (*With You I'm Born Again* with Billy Preston, 1979); 41 US R&B (*Quick Slick*, 1981); 2 UK (*With You I'm Born Again*)

R Dean Taylor

It would appear that British listeners liked what they heard from R Dean Taylor more than their American counterparts did: although *Indiana Wants Me* was a top five hit stateside in 1970, it was the only time he breached the Billboard top 60. In the UK, however, that song was only one of four top 40 hits that started in 1968 with *Gotta See Jane* (number 17), continued with *Indiana Wants Me* and *There's A Ghost In My House* (1974, number three) and finished with *Window Shopping* (1974, number 36). Taylor, still one of few white artists to make it big at Motown, had begun his music career at the age of 12, playing country and rock 'n' roll, and released his first record for Audiomaster in 1960. After moving to the US from his native Canada he cut another couple of singles before coming to Berry Gordy's notice. At Motown he came into his own as a songwriter, joining Eddie Holland to compose, among other smashes, the Supremes' *Love Child*. But Taylor was going places as a performer by 1967, and

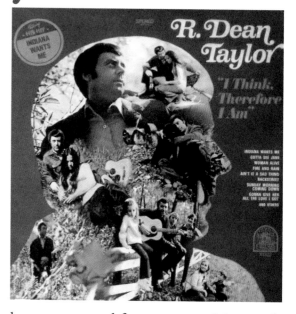

he was a natural for a move to Motown's Rare Earth label when it launched in 1969. Fame on Britain's Northern Soul scene was to follow, and he even returned years after his official retirement to headline shows in the late 90s.

Born: 11 May 1939, Toronto, Ontario
Type: Soul, pop
Highest chart positions: 5 US (*Indiana Wants Me*, 1970); 2 UK (*Indiana Wants Me*)

Teena Marie

You could be forgiven for believing that Mary Christine Brockert, known to music fans as Teena Marie, was of African-American descent, such was the soulfulness of her distinctive R&B voice. Well, she grew up in a largely black neighbourhood and was influenced by the area's matriarch, her godmother Berthalynn Jackson, but she was as white as they come. That was no bar to her landing a job at Motown and then, with the writing and production help of Rick James, releasing a well-received album, *Wild And Peaceful*, on the Gordy label in 1979. A duet with James, *I'm A Sucker For Your Love*, was an R&B hit and stirred interest in Britain, where *Behind The Groove* (1980) took her to number six. Marie's second album, *Lady T*, went gold in the US, as did her third (*Irons In The Fire*, 1980) and fourth (*It Must Be Magic*, 1981). Her biggest Stateside hit, *Lovergirl*, came after she had left Motown, accompanied by some legal nastiness, for Epic. By then she had been writing and producing her own material for some time. Her last album, *Congo Square*, came in 2009 and featured a collaboration with daughter Alia Rose. She died of natural causes in 2010 and among the luminaries attending her funeral were Smokey Robinson and Stevie Wonder.

Left: *Teena Marie – wild and peaceful, yet behind the groove*

Born: 5 March 1956, Santa Monica, California
Died: 26 December 2010, Pasadena, California
Type: R&B, soul, disco, funk, jazz
Highest chart positions: 4 US (*Lovergirl*, 1984); 1 US R&B (*Ooo La La La*, 1988); 6 UK (*Behind The Groove*, 1980)

The Temptations

They're still here, as the title of their 2010 album proclaimed. They're still here after so many dizzying changes in line-up – tenor Otis Williams is the only original who continues to perform – that you're sometimes in danger of forgetting the great Temptations line-ups that bestrode the 60s and 70s like colossi. But come on, could anyone in possession of their faculties really forget such timeless classics as *My Girl*, *Ain't Too Proud To Beg* or *Papa was A*

Rollin' Stone? The Temptations sang and danced their way into the world's affections, mixing pure pop with deep soul and, later, psychedelically tinged funk – and they have never left. It was thanks to the 1961 fusion of two Detroit groups, the Primes and the Distants, that the first Temptations team came together. Otis Williams, Paul Williams (no relation), Elbridge Bryant, Melvin Franklin and Eddie Kendricks formed the Elgins and, after a change of name, clinched a deal at Motown. Single releases on the Miracle label followed but didn't do much. In 1963 Bryant left the group and the following year David Ruffin replaced him. Now things started to motor; after a few minor hits with Smokey Robinson and Ronald White on writing and production duties, they hit the big time with *My Girl* and stayed there. For the next 12 years, until they left Motown for a brief, ill-advised stay with Atlantic, they hardly ever left the top 40, and their career would eventually see them registering 37 top 10 hits. This

Founded: 1961

Origin: Detroit, Michigan

Type: R&B, soul, doo-wop, pop, rock 'n' roll

Members: Elbridge 'Al' Bryant, GC Cameron, Ray Davis, Dennis Edwards, David English, Melvin Franklin, Damon Harris, Barrington 'Bo' Henderson, Joe Herndon, Eddie Kendricks, Glenn Leonard, Harry McGilberry, Cal Osborne, Ricky Owens, Theo Peoples, Louis Price, David Ruffin, Richard Street, Ron Tyson, Terry Weeks, Otis Williams, Paul Williams, Bruce Williamson, Ali-Ollie Woodson

Highest chart positions: 1 US, 1 US R&B (*My Girl*, 1964, *I Can't Get Next To You*, 1969, *Just My Imagination (Running Away With Me)*, 1971); 1 US (*Papa Was A Rollin' Stone*, 1972); 1 US R&B (*The Way You Do The Things You Do*, 1964, *Get Ready, Ain't Too Proud To Beg, Beauty Is Only Skin Deep* and *(I Know) I'm Losing You*, all 1966, *I Wish It Would Rain* and *I Could Never Love Another (After Loving You)*, both 1968, *Runaway Child, Running Wild* and *I Can't Get Next To You*, both 1969, *Masterpiece* and *Let Your Hair Down*, both 1973, *Happy People*, 1974, *Shakey Ground*, 1975); 2 UK (*My Girl*, 1992)

was despite the ups, downs, changes and upsets that are part and parcel of a long-lived group's life. Ruffin was fired in 1968 and replaced by Dennis Edwards, for example, and the group started to specialise in Norman Whitfield-produced political urgings like *Ball Of Confusion*. Kendricks left in 1971, intent on a lucrative solo career. Paul Williams left in the early 70s and later committed suicide. There was that short period away from Motown, and more and ever more personnel changes, with Ruffin and Kendricks returning and then going again. It's been a long, wonderful ride.

Tammi Terrell

Tammi Terrell was only 24 when she died as a result of brain cancer, but she packed a lot into her short life. With Marvin Gaye she made some of musical history's most affecting love duets, and she had a creditable recording career before she even got to Motown. Born Thomasina Montgomery, she was an early starter, as so many Motown stars have been. When she was 13 she was opening for the likes of Patti LaBelle & the Bluebelles and she signed for the Scepter label in 1961. James Brown snapped Terrell up for his Try Me label and she toured with his live show. While she was studying at university she issued *If I Would Marry You* (1964) on Checker. Spotted by Berry Gordy, she signed to Motown and released *I Can't Believe You Love Me* in 1965, but it was when she was partnered with Gaye that things happened, starting with Ashford-Simpson's *Ain't No Mountain High Enough* (1967). Gaye was so broken up by Terrell's death that he gave up touring for three years. The chemistry between

the pair was magical, and the world will always be grateful.

Born: 29 April 1945, Philadelphia, Pennsylvania
Died: 16 March 1970, Philadelphia, Pennsylvania
Type: R&B, soul, pop
Highest chart positions: 5 US, 2 US R&B (*Your Precious Love* with Marvin Gaye, 1967); 1 US R&B (*Ain't Nothing Like The Real Thing* with Marvin Gaye and *You're All I Need To Get By* with Marvin Gaye, both 1968); 9 UK (*The Onion Song* with Marvin Gaye, 1969)

The Undisputed Truth

Producer Norman Whitfield already had a few 'psychedelic soul' hits under his belt – thanks to his pioneering work with the Temptations – when he made *Smiling Faces Sometimes* with the Undisputed Truth, a group he had put together with the express purpose of taking his experiments further. Funky, far-out guitars and socially aware lyrics were the order of the day, with lead singer Joe Harris and Billie Rae Calvin and Brenda Joyce Evans filling in the gaps. The group had just the one big hit, but they were lurking around the lower reaches of the Hot 100 and the R&B and dance charts as late as 1979 with numbers like *You Make Your Own Heaven And Hell Right Here On Earth*, *Papa was A Rollin' Stone* (both 1972), *Mama I Got A Brand New Thing (Don't Say No)* (1973) and *Let's Go Down To The Disco* (1977). Whitfield tended not to go for short, snappy titles. The psychedelic image was emphasised by the group's oversize Afros and white make-up, and the image became even more outlandish as time went on. When Whitfield left Motown to set up his own label, the Undisputed Truth followed and were joined by Rose Royce and Willie Hutch.

Left: *The Undisputed Truth - they made their own heaven and hell right here on Earth*

Founded: 1971
Origin: Detroit, Michigan
Type: R&B, psychedelic soul, funk
Members: Tyrone Berkeley, Taka Boom, Billie Rae Calvin, Tyrone Douglas, Brenda Joyce Evans, Joe Harris, Virginia McDonald, Carl Smalls, Calvin Stephenson
Highest chart positions: 3 US, 2 US R&B (*Smiling Faces Sometimes*, 1971); 43 UK (*You + Me = Love*, 1976)

The Valadiers

Below: *The Valadiers – sadly, they didn't pull up any trees*

Here's yet another first: the Valadiers were the first white group to sign for Motown, all the way back in the early 60s. To be honest, they're noteworthy for just that one reason: they didn't last long and they didn't pull up many trees. The group, taking Jackie Wilson and the Flamingoes as their influences, formed when they were at high school and, as soon as school was finished, auditioned at Motown. Putting their signatures to a three-year contract, they recorded *Nothing Is Going To Change It* and the alarmingly titled *Somebody Help Me Find My Baby* but the recordings were quietly filed away. The next session came up with *Greetings (This Is Uncle Sam)*, which had been written by the group but was not credited to them when it appeared on the Miracle label in 1961. The story of an unwilling draftee into the army during America's Vietnam War was later covered by the Monitors and performed even worse in the charts on that occasion. For the Valadiers, it sold in the Mid-West and the East but sales were negligible outside those regions. The group's next recordings – *When I'm Away* (1962) and *I Found A Girl* (1963) – did not find a place close to label bosses' hearts and that was just about it. The Valadiers disbanded in 1965, although a couple of them remained in the music business.

Founded: 1959
Origin: Detroit, Michigan
Type: R&B, soul, doo-wop
Members: Stuart Avig, Martin Coleman, Art Glasser, Jerry Light
Highest chart position: 89 US (*Greetings (This Is Uncle Sam)*, 1961)

Vanity

Denise Katrina Matthews came out of the project that was Vanity 6 – assembled by Prince at a time when he was a rising star – and recorded two albums for Motown under the name of Vanity. Out of the albums, which did pretty well in the charts, came three singles – *Mechanical Emotion, Pretty Mess* and *Under The Influence* – the last two of which made it into the Hot 100. Then, after a career that had encompassed modelling, dancing and acting as well as singing, not to mention years of drug abuse, Vanity gave it all up. In 1994, while on life support as a result of the effects of smoking crack, she became a born-again Christian and jettisoned the Vanity persona that had brought her trouble. Not only that, she threw out everything that connected her with the music business and declined to receive any further money from her work as Vanity. And she now devotes her time to evangelism, speaking in churches worldwide. Which is a very long way from her life as part of Vanity 6, which

Left: *Vanity – she modelled, she danced, she acted, she sang*

started when the beauty queen and model met Prince Rogers Nelson in 1980. Struck with her beauty and naming her Vanity, the future megastar asked her to front the group he was forming. They became known for their explicit lyrics, raunchy performances and provocative stage costumes, and had a minor hit with the aptly titled *Nasty Girl* (1982). It was some time before she saw the light.

Born: 4 January 1959, Niagara Falls, Ontario
Type: R&B, soul, funk
Highest chart positions: 56 US, 9 US R&B (*Under The Influence*, 1986)

The Velvelettes

It was when Norman Whitfield was assigned to the Velvelettes' case that they found success. It was Whitfield who co-wrote and produced *Needle In A Haystack*, released on Motown's VIP label in the spring of 1964, a year after the group had signed up, and it went on to make number 45 in the US. They had been formed early in the decade by Bertha Barbee, a student at Western Michigan University. She was joined by the 14-year-old Carolyn 'Cal' Gill, Mildred Gill, Norma Barbee and Betty Kelly and together they looked and sounded like the kind of girl group Motown wanted. So they auditioned for the company, with the encouragement of a nephew of Berry Gordy's, Robert Bullock, and were signed in late 1962. Early the following year they started recording with Mickey Stevenson in the producer's chair – and Stevie Wonder playing harmonica – and released *There He Goes* on the IPG label. Following the success of *Needle In A Haystack* came *He Was Really Sayin' Somethin'*, but further chart spots were hard to find. It was well after the group had disbanded that *These Things Will Keep Me Loving You* charted in the UK.

Founded: 1961
Origin: Detroit, Michigan
Type: R&B, soul, pop
Members: Bertha Barbee, Norma Barbee, Cal Gill, Mildred Gill, Betty Kelly, Annette McMillan, Sandra Tilley
Highest chart positions: 45 US (*Needle In A Haystack*, 1964); 21 US R&B (*He Was Really Sayin' Somethin'*, 1965); 34 UK (*These Things Will Keep Me Loving You*, 1971)

Junior Walker

Junior Walker's rasping, honking, bleeping sax was the mainstay of his group, the Allstars, from their first Hot 100 appearance in 1965 until 1979, when *Wishing On A Star* became their last single to make waves on the R&B chart. In between came a long run of dancefloor-fillers that were almost as popular in Britain as they were in the States. They were often instrumental covers of numbers that had been hits for other Motown artists – *How Sweet It Is (To Be Loved By You)*, *Money (That's What I Want)* (both 1966), and *Come See About Me* (1967), for example. Walker, born Autry DeWalt Mixon Jr, took up the saxophone and formed his first group, the Jumping Jacks, in his teens. The Junior Walker stage name came from a childhood nickname. In 1961 Harvey Fuqua signed him to his Harvey label, where he laid down the template for what was to follow: sax-led, beat-filled instrumentals that set fingers popping. By 1964 Fuqua and Walker were at Motown and in 1965 came his first smash hit, *Shotgun*, produced by Berry Gordy. Holland-Dozier-Holland later came on board to oversee the cover versions, and it all went swimmingly until Walker left Motown for the Whitfield label in 1979.

Left: *Junior Walker – produced, with his Allstars, a long stream of dancefloor-fillers*

Born: 14 June 1931, Blytheville, Arkansas
Died: 23 November 1995, Battle Creek, Michigan
Type: R&B, soul, funk
Highest chart positions: 4 US, 1 US R&B (*Shotgun*, 1965, *What Does It Take (To Win Your Love)*, 1969); 12 UK ((*I'm A) Road Runner*, 1966)

Grover Washington Jr

GROVER WASHINGTON JR

Below: *Grover Washington – one of the progenitors of smooth jazz*

Grover Washington Jr was able to switch saxophones, from soprano to alto to tenor and baritone, just as readily as he was able to change musical styles, excelling in all of them. Equally at home playing squalling, thumping R&B and soul numbers and more experimental jazzy workouts, he was one of the musicians who gave rise to the smooth jazz genre that has found so many followers. He started his musical explorations at the age of 10 and from 1959 to 1963 toured with the Four Clefs. After a spell of freelancing came the army, then a 1967 move to Philadelphia, and his break came in 1971 when Hank Crawford failed to show for a recording for the Kudu label. As Crawford's replacement, Washington came up with the album *Inner City Blues*, released on Motown, and was on his way. It was a big seller and an influential record, and he followed it with *All The King's Horses* (1972, Verve label), *Soul Box* and *Soul Box, Vol 2* (both 1972, both Motown). Singles from the albums were finding R&B and pop fans, and in 1981 he nearly made it to the top of the pops with the Bill Withers collaboration *Just The Two Of Us*. Washington suffered a fatal heart attack in 1999; far too early.

Born: 12 December 1943, Buffalo, New York
Died: 17 December 1999, New York City, New York
Type: Jazz, R&B, soul
Highest chart positions: 2 US, 3 US R&B (*Just The Two Of Us* featuring Bill Withers, 1981); 34 UK (*Just The Two Of Us*)

Mary Wells

Until she left the label in 1964, when she was riding high on a wave of popularity, Mary Wells was Motown's hottest property. Coming to public notice as early as 1960 with *Bye Bye Baby*, she had helped to form the Motown sound and put the company on the right road to the sunlit uplands it would one day occupy. A long succession of brilliant hit singles, culminating in the monumental success of *My Guy*, confirmed her position as the First Lady of Motown, but then it all went sour. It was a tragedy for a woman who had already had her share of troubles: contracting spinal meningitis at the age of two, she suffered partial blindness and deafness and temporary paralysis. Music proved to be a healer, and by the time she was 10, Wells was singing in Detroit nightclubs. Discarding teenage plans to become a scientist, she followed the example of other Detroit musicians and approached Berry Gordy, offering him a song she'd written with Jackie Wilson in mind. Instead, she found herself in the studio recording the song, *Bye Bye Baby*. It's said that 22 takes were required, but eventually Wells nailed it and the song was released on Motown in September 1960, rising to number 45 on the Hot 100. Her career had got off to a flyer and she was on her way to becoming the label's first female star. Soon she was working with Mickey Stevenson on *I Don't Want To Take A Chance* (1961) and with Smokey Robinson on *The One Who Really*

Above: *Mary Wells – My Guy propelled her into uncharted territory*

Loves You (1962), her first very big hit. The song, written and produced by Smokey, climbed to number eight on the pop chart and the Wells-Robinson partnership was established; it went on to triumph with songs like *You Beat Me To The Punch*, *Two Lovers*, *Laughing Boy* and *Your Old Standby*. Holland-Dozier-Holland stepped in to write and produce *You Lost The Sweetest Boy* and its B-side, *What's Easy For Two Is So Hard For One* (1963), both of which charted, and then it was back to Robinson. His song *My Guy*, released in Mach 1964, propelled Wells to unprecedented territory: top of the Billboard Hot 100 and number five in the UK. Although she would never reach as high again on the British side of the Atlantic, *My Guy* was enough to earn Wells a lifelong reputation for excellence in Britain, helped by the Beatles' declaration that she was their favourite American singer. Sadly, her time at the top was nearly up. A duet with Marvin Gaye, *Once Upon A Time*, kept her in the charts, but it was her last hit. In dispute with Motown over the whereabouts of moneys from *My Guy*, she left for 20th Century Fox amid rumours of impending film roles. They never came. When Wells died as a result of throat cancer in 1992, her passing was mourned bitterly worldwide.

Born: 13 May 1943, Detroit, Michigan
Died: 26 July 1992, Los Angeles, California
Type: R&B, soul, pop, disco
Highest chart positions: 1 US, 1 US R&B (*My Guy*, 1964); 1 US R&B (*You Beat Me To The Punch*, 1962, *Two Lovers*, 1963); 5 UK (*My Guy*)

Kim Weston

Many Motown stars started out singing in a church choir, but few started as early as Agatha Nathalia Weston, better known as Kim of that ilk. She was just three years old when she first gave voice to her praise for the Lord, and she was in her teens when she joined a travelling gospel group. Twenty-two when she signed with Motown, Weston notched up a minor hit with *Love Me All The Way* (1963) but bigger and better things were to come. The following year she began to duet with Marvin Gaye, and *What Good Am I Without You* made its way to number 61 on the Hot 100. Next came a version of a Holland-Dozier-Holland song that had already been recorded by Eddie Holland; Weston's version of *Take Me In Your Arms (Rock Me A Little While)*, released in September 1965, continued her progress by reaching number 50, and four on the R&B chart. In 1966 came a slight backwards step in the shape of *Helpless*, but all was set to rights when another performance with Gaye, *It Takes Two* (written by her husband, Mickey Stevenson, and Sylvia Moy) breached the top 20 and founds fans in Britain too. Motown took the view that Gaye would do even better duetting with Tammi Terrell, and Weston (and Stevenson) left Motown in 1967.

Left: *Kim Weston – it took two with Marvin Gaye*

Born: 20 December 1939, Detroit, Michigan
Type: R&B, soul
Highest chart positions: 14 US, 4 US R&B (*It Takes Two* with Marvin Gaye, 1967); 4 US R&B (*Take Me In Your Arms (Rock Me A Little While)*, 1965); 16 UK (*It Takes Two*)

Bruce Willis

Not many screen fans expected Bruce Willis to pop up in the music charts, but that's what happened in early 1987 when *Respect Yourself* ascended all the way to number five on the Billboard Hot 100. It seemed Willis had a decent voice and a love of old rock 'n' roll and R&B numbers, and wasn't just a thespian who would go on to die hard, die harder and, possibly, die even harder than that. You see, the vocal talents of Mr Willis, star of the comedy-drama TV series *Moonlighting*, had been noticed when he recorded some wine cooler commercials, and Motown couldn't wait to get him into a studio. The hit came from the resultant album *The Return Of Bruno*, for the recording of which Willis received the help of legendary musicians like the Temptations, Booker T Jones, Siedah Garrett and Ruth Pointer. It contained the Leiber-Stoller-Pomus song *Young Blood* (also a hit single), the 1964 Drifters hit *Under The Boardwalk* (a hit for Willis in America and Britain), Allen Toussaint's *Fun Time* and *Secret Agent Man* (a Johnny Rivers version of which had been used for the opening titles of the American broadcast of the British TV spy series *Danger Man*). Motown and Willis attempted to repeat the dose with a further album, *If It Don't Kill You, It Just Makes You Stronger* in 1989, but it seems fans had heard enough.

Born: 19 March 1955, Idar-Oberstein, Rhineland-Palatinate
Type: R&B, soul, rock 'n' roll
Highest chart positions: 5 US, 20 US R&B (*Respect Yourself*, 1987); 2 UK (*Under The Boardwalk*, 1987)

Stevie Wonder

It's as futile to try to categorise Stevie Wonder as it is to attempt to count the stars in the sky. Why would you want to, anyway? What we have in Stevie Wonder is genius, pure and simple; genius that has allowed him to make magnificent music in whatever style he has turned his hand to, and captivate generations of listeners. He produced exquisite work from an age when many people are still learning to read. And to his credit, he's a one-label man: he has remained loyal to Motown his entire life. Born Stevland Hardaway Judkins six weeks prematurely, Wonder was blind almost from birth, a fact that some people believe gave him an intensified awareness of sound and its colours. Moving to Detroit when he was four, he had his name changed to Morris and began learning to play a wide range of instruments, piano, harmonica, drums and bass guitar among them. He had mastered them by the time he was nine, and it wasn't long before he came to Berry Gordy's notice. Gordy was beguiled by the boy sensation and in 1961 signed him to Tamla under the name of Little Stevie Wonder. His first single, *I Call It Pretty Music, But The Old People Call It The Blues*, was released later that year and two albums were issued in 1962, but it was in 1963 that his first hit single struck with the force of a tempest. *Fingertips – Part 1 & 2*, recorded live at a show in Chicago, showcased the boy wonder's virtuosity on harmonica, bongos and vocals, and surged to the top of the charts. The

Below: *Stevie Wonder – first Berry Gordy and then the world were beguiled by the boy sensation*

Above: *Stevie Wonder – an example of a rarity, a one-label man*

Born: 13 May 1950, Saginaw, Michigan
Type: R&B, soul, pop, funk, jazz
Highest chart positions: 1 US, 1 US R&B (*Fingertips – Part 1 & 2*, 1963, *Superstition*, 1972, *You Haven't Done Nothin'* with The Jackson 5, 1974, *I Wish*, 1976, *Sir Duke*, 1977, *I Just Called To Say I Love You*, 1984, *Part-Time Lover* and *That's What Friends Are For* with Dionne Warwick, Gladys Knight and Elton John, both 1985); 1 US (*You Are The Sunshine Of My Life*, 1973, *Ebony And Ivory* with Paul McCartney, 1982); 1 US R&B (*Uptight (Everything's Alright)*, 1965, *Blowin' In The Wind*, 1966, *I Was Made To Love Her*, 1967, *Shoo-Be-Doo-Be-Doo-Da-Day*, 1968, *Signed, Sealed, Delivered I'm Yours*, 1970, *Higher Ground* and *Living For The City*, both 1973, *Boogie On Reggae Woman*, 1974, *Master Blaster (Jammin')*, 1980, *That Girl*, 1981, *Skeletons*, 1987, *You Will Know*, 1988); 1 UK (*Ebony And Ivory*, *I Just Called To Say I Love You*)

13-year-old thus became the youngest performer to top the Billboard Hot 100. There then followed one of music's most stellar careers, some of whose landmarks are recorded on these pages. He has had more than 30 top 10 hits in the United States and 17 in Britain; received 22 Grammy Awards; made albums, like *Talking Book* (1972), *Innervisions* (1973) and *Songs In The Key Of Life* (1976), that are among the finest musical works man has made; and through it all exhibited a love of life and his fellow humans that has always exhilarated.

Zhané

Zhané, part of Queen Latifah's Flavor Unit collective, made the most of their first chance to record. The duo produced *Hey Mr DJ* for the 1993 compilation album *Roll Wit Tha Flava* (which also featured the likes of Latifah, Freddie Foxxx, Apache, D-Nice and Naughty By Nature) and, although it was the last track on the CD, it went on to be a massive hip hop hit. Jamaican Renee Neufville and Rhode Island native Jean Norris-Baylor earned themselves a deal with Motown and went on to make two well-regarded albums – *Pronounced Jah-Nay* (1994) and *Saturday Night* (1997) – and a series of hit singles. The first album, which sold over a million copies in America, gave rise to three hits besides *Hey Mr DJ*: *Groove Thang*, *Sending My Love* and *Vibe*, the first two of which were big on the R&B charts. Zhané went on to record for film soundtracks and work with Busta Rhymes, De La Soul and Naughty By Nature, both activities that brought them further success in the charts. Their second album

Left: *Zhané's Jean-Norris Baylor – rolled, with others, wit tha flava*

was less productive in terms of sales and hit singles, but it did supply *Request Line*, which turned out to be their best-known tune in the UK. They disbanded in 1999 but both members have gone on to make a mark as individuals.

Founded: 1993

Origin: Philadelphia, Pennsylvania

Type: R&B, soul, new jack swing, hip hop, dance

Members: Renee Neufville, Jean Norris-Baylor

Highest chart positions: 6 US (*Hey Mr DJ*, 1993); 2 US R&B (*Groove Thang*, 1994); 22 UK (*Request Line*, 1997)

ALSO AVAILABLE IN THE PLAYER BY PLAYER SERIES

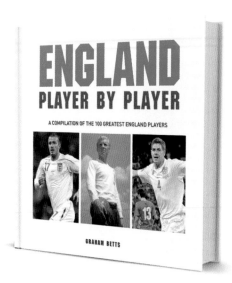

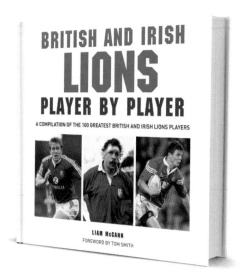

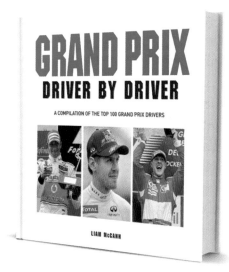

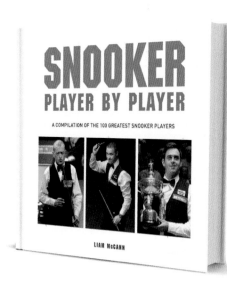

ALSO AVAILABLE IN THE PLAYER BY PLAYER SERIES

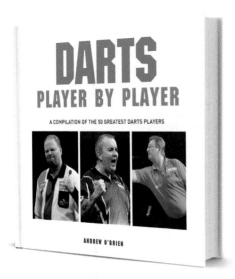

DARTS
PLAYER BY PLAYER

A COMPILATION OF THE 50 GREATEST DARTS PLAYERS

ANDREW O'BRIEN

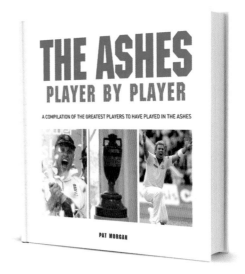

THE ASHES
PLAYER BY PLAYER

A COMPILATION OF THE GREATEST PLAYERS TO HAVE PLAYED IN THE ASHES

PAT MORGAN

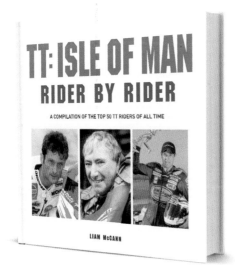

TT: ISLE OF MAN
RIDER BY RIDER

A COMPILATION OF THE TOP 50 TT RIDERS OF ALL TIME

LIAM McCANN

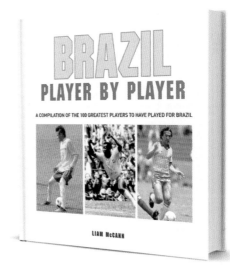

BRAZIL
PLAYER BY PLAYER

A COMPILATION OF THE 100 GREATEST PLAYERS TO HAVE PLAYED FOR BRAZIL

LIAM McCANN

The pictures in this book were provided courtesy of the following:

GETTY IMAGES
101 Bayham Street, London NW1 0AG

WIKICOMMONS
commons.wikimedia.org

Design & Artwork by Scott Giarnese

Published by G2 Entertainment Limited

Publishers: Jules Gammond & Edward Adams

Written by Pat Morgan